Prais
Indie Writi

"*Indie Writing Wisdom* has just about everything that I learned after-the-fact when it came to publishing my debut novel. Inspiring, insightful and invaluable…there's so much here for every would-be published author. You won't regret picking this one up!"

B.T. KEATON,
author of the award-winning novel *Transference*

"I could have saved a lot of time if this book had existed when I first started researching self-publishing and book marketing. This is a must-read for all new indie authors or for authors in general who are struggling with marketing or want to appear more professional."

FELICIA BLAEDEL,
author of *Chasing Pebbles*

"The best introduction to self-publishing resource you could ever own. This anthology of sorts was extremely professionally written by its contributors and put together by its creator Samantha Goodwin in the name of awareness of Encephalitis. If you are looking for a real and authentic look into the world of self-publishing then this book is for you."

BECKA YAEGER,
Founder of Becka's Best Author Services,
www.beckasbest.com

"Most books tell you how to get noticed. This one showed me. You don't need anything bar your inspiration, and this book!"

TRACIE DAILY,
author of *Checkmate* and *Tracie's Story*

"This is a must-have handbook for every new and upcoming indie author, assembled together by authors themselves. Their combination of knowledge and insight into the world of writing and the self-publishing industry goes without saying; they offer invaluable advice and suggestions drawn from their own experiences and supported with ideas and links to make the process easier for you.

If you are serious about writing a book, then don't delay, buy and read well in advance of writing your manuscript as this could be your new best friend. There is so much more involved than just writing and publishing a book, and it is easy to get lost in what can only be described as a minefield."

DONNA H. DUHIG,
author of *In The End*

"*Indie Writing Wisdom* is amazingly insightful. An author never stops learning their craft and improving their skills, and this is the perfect book to help you. Whether you are just starting out, or have already published multiple books, I can guarantee that you will find it extremely useful and enlightening. I've taken lots of notes and have already implemented some of the suggestions within the planning of my next project.

The chapters within *Indie Writing Wisdom* are extremely easy to digest and cover a great range of topics. The authors who have contributed to the book are well practiced and skilled in their chosen subject and that shines through with the quality of the advice that they share."

J.D. GROOM,
author of *Sorceress of Truth*

"*Indie Writing Wisdom* is a comprehensive, beginners guide to self-publishing for new indie authors. It has a wide array of advice on various topics such as writing, editing, and even marketing.

While it's impossible for a single book to address all of these topics completely, *Indie Writing Wisdom* provides a wonderful starting point for anyone who is new to self-publishing. The advice is professional, straightforward, and applicable to both new and veteran self-published authors. It will surely give readers the boost they need to know that self-publishing is not only possible but can be amazing if you know what to do."

CLAERIE KAVANAUGH,
author of the *Duet Rubato* series and *Queen of Thieves*

"This was genuinely such an interesting read.
Each chapter is written by a different experienced writer and gives a step-by-step guide authors should take from beginning to end of the self-publishing process. Plot structure, editing, formatting, cover design, marketing, building a business – it's all in there.

As an indie author myself, I found this to be a practical view of the writer's craft. Everything is written clearly and I enjoyed each writer's personal anecdotes about their experiences. There is so much in this book that I wish I had known before publishing my first novel and so much I am still able to take away now. It's an invaluable source when it comes to being an author. What's even better is all of the profits from the sales will go directly to the Encephalitis Society, in memory of Samantha Goodwin's late father who had the original idea for this book.
I absolutely recommend this – the perfect book for any writer."

S.M. YAIR-LEVY
author of *The Collectors* series

INDIE WRITING WISDOM

**Practical advice and inspiring insights
on writing and self-publishing**

Candice Bellows • Tempeste Blake • Shauntay Dunbar • Samantha Goodwin
Marie Landry • Holly Lyne • Stephen McClellan • Michelle Raab
Julia Scott • Angeline Trevena • Kara S. Weaver

ISBN: 9798699476046

First published in 2020 by Amazon Kindle Direct Publishing (KDP).

Also available as an e-book.

For everyone who ever dreamt of writing a book.

Contents

Introduction
by Samantha Goodwin

Where It All Began

When I first started writing my debut novel something that I found extremely helpful was reading advice from more experienced authors to learn what had worked for them and, perhaps more importantly, what pitfalls to avoid. But, invariably all of this sage advice came from very disjointed sources: blogs, Facebook groups, author interviews, social media, the list goes on… I couldn't help thinking it would be so much easier to have a writing anthology of sorts, collating all the best advice from a number of different authors in one central reference book.

And so *Indie Writing Wisdom* was born.

A Truly Global Collaboration

A wide range of well-respected indie authors have contributed to this book who hail from all over the world including the United States, Canada, the United Kingdom and the Netherlands. Not to mention we have also involved beta readers from Australia, Denmark and New Zealand.

Together, we have shared all of our best tips about what worked for us to produce our books to the highest possible standard, plan an effective launch and actually make sales. Our hope is that our advice will help to inspire the next generation of writers, or indeed help fellow indie authors who are seeking ideas about how to leverage the exposure of their new or existing books and make more sales. There are many pearls of wisdom for you to discover, all of which should help you to successfully navigate the daunting process of self-publishing.

Indie or Traditional?

If you're toying with the idea of becoming an indie author, but still feel inclined to query first to attempt becoming traditionally published, then that's great. Be assured this book is crammed full of useful advice that will help you to craft the best novel possible, regardless of which publishing route you eventually take.

Remember that you should always approach a literary agent or publisher only after you have polished your manuscript to the very best of your abilities. Then you are truly giving yourself the best chance of success. All the early chapters should help you with this process. In fact, some of the contributors are hybrid authors themselves, with both indie and traditionally published books to their names, so hearing about their experiences should be suitably enlightening.

What About Genre?

If you're wondering if the content contained within this book is relevant to your genre, then believe me, it is! All of this writing and self-publishing advice transcends genre and is equally applicable, regardless of what type of story you are creating. Testament to that fact, the contributing authors cover an impressive range of genres with their own books: young adult, fantasy, science fiction, contemporary, crime, romance, dystopia, comedy, urban fantasy, post-apocalyptic, romantic suspense, supernatural, Christian fiction, non-fiction, short stories and children's picture books. Collectively, we have released 60 books to date over the past decade, so we have a wealth of experience to share.

Did I Mention This Is All for Charity?

To further celebrate the indie book community, a number of talented bookstagrammers have contributed some stunning original photographs for this book. Plus, this is all in the name of charity too. Every single penny of profit from both the paperback and e-book sales of *Indie Writing Wisdom* is being donated to the Encephalitis Society (the brain inflammation charity). I had no idea this devastating neurological condition even existed before it suddenly claimed the life of my dad when he was just 62, robbing him of the chance to meet his grandchildren. You can find out more about the condition in the final chapter, 'Encephalitis.'

Think Positive

It would be amiss not to also mention that the contributing authors all wrote their chapters in isolation in their respective countries during the lockdowns related to the global COVID-19 pandemic in 2020. At a dark time when it would have been easy to have a bleak outlook, I was so heartened to collaborate with other like-minded authors who chose instead to pour their energy into something positive. This book is one of the ways we chose to give back to others.

To all the writers reading these words, this is for you. The world needs your book. We hope you enjoy the read.

Motivation Matters
by Stephen McClellan

What Is All This Motivation Fuss About?

A Lamborghini is one of the most expensive cars in the world, ranging from hundreds of thousands to millions of dollars in cost. In fact, most lists rank at least one model of a Lamborghini as one of the top three most expensive cars in the world. But let me tell you something – all that horse-power, speed and sleek design means nothing if the car doesn't have fuel in it. It may look beautiful and be marvelled at and bragged about to the neighbours, but if the car doesn't have fuel for its engine, it's not leaving the driveway.

This is why motivation is so important. **Motivation is the fuel that drives your writing**. Without it, you will be stuck, immobile, possibly pretty to look at, but ultimately, you will go nowhere. Because the harsh reality is that you can have all the tools, from experience and knowledge to raw talent, but if you don't have something that continues to refuel those areas, then you will eventually be left stranded with no place to go.

Now, you may be tempted to say, 'I'm fine, Stephen. I get inspired by ideas all the time, so I don't need help staying motivated.' But be careful. Inspiration is different than motivation. Inspiration *gets* you going, while motivation *keeps* you going. If inspiration is the match, then motivation is the firewood. Inspiration is temporary, but motivation can be permanent. This is because inspiration is rooted in feelings and emotions, while moti-vation is rooted in established mindsets and principles. It's crucial that we don't get these two words confused.

So, does it matter? Trust me when I say, yes, motivation matters.

What Is the Key to Staying Motivated?

Before we continue, I should probably tell you that the insights in this chapter are primarily about mindset, rather than mechanics. I will conclude with some practical tips to help you stay on the right track and practice self-accountability, but in the first instance it is far more important to properly understand the source of your motivation, as that underpins everything you do.

Now, let's get to it. Notice I didn't title this section, 'What is the key to *getting* motivated?' I asked, 'What is the key to *staying* motivated?' Once again, inspiration gets you moving, but motivation keeps you moving. So, how do you maintain the right mindset to stay motivated? It's not necessarily easy, but it is straightforward.

If you ask a motivational speaker (or a person with any level of success) how to stay motivated, they will ask the question that most likely we have all heard before; 'What's your why?' Or otherwise stated, 'What's the reason behind why you do what you do?' It's an excellent question and one I agree with wholeheartedly. But I think there is more to it. Because if you really think about it, what that question is really asking is, 'Why do you believe you *want* to do what you are doing?' or 'Why do you believe you *should* do what you are doing?' And by definition, another word for a strong held belief is *conviction*.

So, I think we need to morph the question a bit. Instead of asking, 'What's your why?' I think the question that needs to be asked is, 'What's your conviction?' I say this because when people talk about reasons why they do something, they can be casual, surface level or in some cases even petty. But when people discuss their convictions, the conversation goes a layer deeper, stretches further and establishes a more intricate motive for why they are pursuing their endeavours. So, what is the key to staying motivated? You must answer the question, 'What's your conviction?'

How Do I Establish My Conviction?

There are several different categories that a conviction could fall under, but I'm narrowing it down to two main themes: intrinsic and extrinsic. Which one do you fall under? Let's find out…

Intrinsic

An intrinsic conviction correlates to your inner conscience or what is naturally and organically known about yourself. It is a self-awareness or knowledge that you were meant to do something. It might be a passion that brings you fulfilment and joy like nothing else does, or it may be a talent you innately feel like you have always been gifted with. An intrinsic conviction isn't something that was necessarily taught to you or that you were persuaded to believe. It is the feeling that your spirit won't let you rest or be at peace until you pursue that specific vision. It propels you, drives you, and eats away at you until you are forced to address it.

This is the conviction for many people – they simply 'just know.' People whose conviction is intrinsic stay motivated because they have an unwavering belief that they are doing what they were born to do. In the context of writing a book, you could feel you were always destined to become an author because writing is such a fundamental part of who you are and allows you to express yourself in a way nothing else does, bringing you unparalleled enjoyment. If this is you, then that's absolutely incredible. But if you don't fall into this category, then most likely you relate more to the second category of conviction – the extrinsic.

Extrinsic

An extrinsic conviction could be stated as 'everything else.' Meaning, it is going to correlate to forces outside of yourself and things that are physical by nature. It is going to be something tangible and real, a goal in which growth and progress can be measured. It is typically dedicated to a purpose far greater than yourself. People with an extrinsic conviction pursue their goals for a specific reason that goes beyond a feeling, an awareness or a knowledge that it is what they were simply meant to do.

What does this look like in practice? It could be:

- A **writer** who wants to allow kids to get lost in another world in an attempt to teach them how to dream and envision as well as use their creativity to create a different future.
- A **teacher** who wants to impact and educate young minds who are growing into the next generation of society.
- A **lawyer** who loves the law and takes pride in seeing people treated fairly and justice brought to particular situations.
- **Or it could be to serve in an area** that focuses on improving hunger, poverty, war or any other social justice cause. People whose conviction is extrinsic stay motivated because they live with a sense that they are a part of a bigger vision and investing in a cause that will change humanity for the better.

Now, the reality is that most people's convictions are a little of both – they inwardly believe there is something they were meant to accomplish as well as a physical area in which they want to make an impact. I would venture to say that the most influential leaders today have both an intrinsic as well as an extrinsic conviction that pushes them to pursue their visions. The most important thing to remember, however, is that whether your conviction is intrinsic, extrinsic or a hybrid of both, you need to make sure you have established it.

The Three I Left Out

Notice I didn't mention three words in particular: *money, fame* and *popularity*. I left these out intentionally because you have to be extremely careful not to be fooled by them. After all, they are our greatest temptations as a society because they bring false feelings of worth, value and identity.

These three things in themselves are not necessarily bad, and they can even be a by-product of an intrinsic or extrinsic conviction, but if your motive is strictly to get rich, become famous or be well known, then I will tell you what will happen: either you won't achieve your goal or you will achieve it, but you will achieve *success* rather than *significance*. Success fuelled by the wrong motive is typically represented by selfishness (all about us), whereas significance fuelled by the right motive is typically represented by selflessness (all about other people). At the very least, you are much more likely to have a positive outcome if you are selfless enough to be focused entirely on creating the best book possible for your readers, rather than simply chasing fame and fortune as an author. Like I said, you can still gain money, fame and popularity by pursuing your goal, but they shouldn't *be* your goal.

So where does that leave us? Let's say you have evaluated your talents, passions, gifts and abilities and you are convinced you have a strong conviction of why you are doing what you are doing. What then? Well…what's left is to test it out.

How Do You Know If Your Conviction Is Legitimate?

There are two ways I believe you can assess whether or not the conviction you have established is legitimate or 'the real deal.'

1) Your Conviction Instils Value Into People

I firmly believe your conviction needs to impact humanity in a positive way. It doesn't have to be monumental or earth-shattering, but it should in some way be rooted in bettering the lives of society as a whole, locally as well as globally.

This can take many different forms. For some authors it may be as simple as having a moral message that they want to communicate in their story, in the hope it will make readers stop and think and perhaps even readdress their behaviour or priorities in life.

2) Your Conviction Has Stood Up Against Adversity

This means that it has been tested, knocked around, beat up in the ring and it hasn't surrendered. If you have faced some type of obstacle, setback, discouragement or unforeseen circumstance and it forced you to crumble, walk away or give up on your writing career altogether, then one of two things happened: either you weren't meant for that profession or you never properly established your conviction. One of the greatest predictors of whether or not we have a strong foundation is to observe how it holds up in times of adversity. Think back to a difficult time in your writing journey and reflect on how you reacted. If your resolve crumbled, then it's time to get back to the drawing board.

Coincidentally, they say it takes a village to write a book and that very much rings true. While writing is usually an individual pursuit, that doesn't mean you have to go at it alone. Many new authors find solidarity in seeking out a supportive writing community, whether that is a local writing club or an international writing group. While ultimately maintaining your conviction is down to you, there is benefit in receiving helpful advice and learning about useful coping methods from more experienced authors who have faced obstacles and setbacks in the past.

What Does a Practical Example Look Like?

I'll go first and tell you how I have applied these principles to my own life. When it comes to my conviction, I'm a hybrid of both intrinsic and extrinsic. A friend once asked me, 'How did you know that writing was what you were supposed to be doing?' I answered him, 'Because I got to the place where I couldn't *not* write.' That's where the intrinsic side comes in concerning my writing career. I live with an overwhelming conviction that there are words and stories placed inside of me that will not let me rest until I introduce them to the world. It goes beyond a feeling; it's a self-awareness of who I am and who I was created to be. It could be labelled as a calling, a purpose or fate. Regardless, all I know is that it exists and it's real. Beyond those intrinsic realisations, however, there is an extrinsic component as well.

Like I said before, I believe that our convictions need to instil value into people. The author and speaker John C. Maxwell said it like this – the purpose of life is to 'find yourself' and 'lose yourself.'[1] He said when you *find yourself*, you discover your talents and passions or the things that bring you the most fulfilment and the greatest joy. On the other hand, when you *lose yourself*, you take those talents and passions and reinvest them into areas where external factors are involved (or into people). He said that many people find themselves, but they never learn how to lose themselves. In other words, they have never taken what they have been given and reinvested it into a cause that is greater than themselves.

So, with those thoughts in mind, I reflected on how I could give back and what I could do with the talents, passions, gifts and abilities that I believed God had given me. That's when my vision was born. I decided to dedicate each book I write to a different local or global humanitarian project and reinvest all the royalties I earn from that book into a particular organisation or ministry – all with my goal in mind, *so others may dream*.

The reality is that millions of children all over the world are never given the opportunity to pursue their passions, develop their potential or discover their purpose. Sickness, death, war, abandonment – the circumstances surrounding them have stripped away any chance they have at discovering who they are and why they were created. Or you could say that their circumstances have stripped away any chance they have at even dreaming of a better life. That's where my extrinsic conviction comes into play. Why do I have a conviction to do what I do? *So others may dream.*

---

[1] John C. Maxwell, *Intentional Living: Choosing a Life That Matters*, Published 6 October 2015 by Center Street

How Have My Convictions Influenced My Own Author Journey?

My debut indie novel, *To Dance*, was published in December 2018, and my debut children's picture book, *The Bat and the Mule*, is set to be traditionally published in the spring of 2021. Both of the books have unique roots to how they were formed and the road they took to publication.

To Dance

To Dance was never meant to be a full-length novel. It was originally a two-page children's story about a boy experiencing pain and racial injustice. A friend read the pages and encouraged me to make a short story out of it. After some thought, I turned it into a journal entry style, 13,000-word short story. But then my wife read the piece and said, 'I just want to know what happens to the boy's mother.' That convinced me to write a second part to the story as a Christmas gift to her. What popped out was a 60,000-word manuscript exploring themes of coping with pain, making sense of tragedy and finding significance in suffering.

And why didn't I give up during that time or grow frustrated with the process of countless rounds of revisions?

Two reasons:

- I was convinced that there were people who needed to hear the messages of hope and healing that the book contained.
- Because of the organisation the book was representing.

I decided to reinvest all the royalties of *To Dance* into an organisation called Compassion First.[2] Based out of Indonesia, they focus on eradicating sex-trafficking in Southeast Asia. Their team rescues girls who have been enslaved, offers them counselling and recovery services, equips them with basic life skills and education and reintroduces them into society. Reminding myself that the success of *To Dance* could literally mean the difference between life and death for innocent girls across the world was the only motivation I needed to see the project through to completion.

---

[2] Visit www.compassionfirst.org to learn more about this charitable organisation.

The Bat and the Mule

My debut children's book is about a bat and a mule that are travelling the same path but see the world from completely different perspectives. Their inability to see each other's viewpoint drives a wedge between them that threatens to destroy any kind of lasting friendship. I was fortunate enough to be offered a contract from a small, traditional publishing house, which was incredible!

However, that was only after a few minor setbacks. And when I say minor, I mean that *The Bat and the Mule* was rejected twelve times from nine different publishers before it was accepted. In fact, I had submitted several different children's books and had been rejected 25 times from eleven different publishers before I landed my first contract.

Once again, why didn't I wave the white flag and surrender? The same two reasons as *To Dance*:

• I was convinced that there were children who needed to hear the messages of kindness, acceptance and understanding that the book conveyed.
• Because of the organisation the book was representing.

The royalties from *The Bat and the Mule* are being reinvested to support the OVI Healthcare organisation.[3] Their founding site in Kenya, the OVI Children's Hospital, takes orphans off the street who are dying of life-threatening illnesses and diseases and offers them the medical attention they need to help nourish them back to health. Aside from the children's hospital, OVI Healthcare is also in the process of opening three more non-profit hospitals in Bangladesh. Through their outpatient clinics, rehabilitation centres and outreach camps, these hospitals will provide healthcare to various socially vulnerable and underserved regions of the country.

In the cases of both books, I could have given up at any time throughout the writing or publication process, but I didn't. Why? Because not only had I established an intrinsic and extrinsic conviction that pursued the hearts of people, but my convictions had been built on a solid foundation that when battle-tested, had not crumbled.

That is my hope for you; that you will establish a conviction that motivates you to see beyond your circumstances and envision a future worth living. You owe it to yourself, as well as to the generations who will come after you. So close your eyes, breathe deep and reflect on what this journey is all about. You won't regret it.

What Does This Mean in Practice?

So, you've identified the source of your motivation and are raring to go – great! But even the best of us can have days when we lack the drive to keep going. Plus, the daunting task of writing a full-length novel can feel a little overwhelming at times.

Therefore, building positive writing habits into your daily life and equipping yourself with some helpful tools and a strong support network can help give you the best chance of success. Remember your motivation is *why* you are writing, but *how* you actually go about coming up with the words is up to you. There is no right or wrong way. Find what works for you and learn how to stick with it.

---

[3] Visit www.ovihospital.org to learn more about this charitable organisation.

Define Your Goals

I would suggest a helpful starting point can be to determine attainable goals that can be broken down into realistic, short-term targets. This can be useful for maintaining momentum in finishing your novel, which is particularly true for when you are working on the stages that you are less enthralled with, such as the editing process. Some authors swear by committing to daily goals and monitoring their progress, such as by tracking wordcounts in an Excel spreadsheet or jotting notes in a writing journal.

Set Aside Time to Write

You know yourself better than anyone else, so you probably already have a good idea of how you could best commit to writing regularly while managing your other responsibilities. Think of your creativity as a muscle that needs to be constantly toned.

To use a fitness analogy: some people are obsessed with cramming in short twenty-minute workout sessions whenever they have the opportunity, others prefer the more structured approach of having scheduled exercise classes or gym sessions booked in, while others require an intensive week-long bootcamp to get them started. The same is true for writers: there will be those that thrive by having a daily wordcount target that they tackle in short bursts, whereas others prefer regular, planned writing time or benefit from attending a writing retreat. Every author will have their own strategy, but what is important is the ongoing dedication to setting aside time for writing and protecting those precious hours in your diary.

Top Tip: Removing distractions is key to staying focused and boosting your productivity. If you lack the discipline to turn off your phone or leave it in another room, you may be interested to learn that there are apps which temporarily block social media, and even the internet, for a specified time window. Examples include Cold Turkey Blocker, FocusMe and Offtime.

Consider Your Writing Environment

Every person's ideal writing environment will be different, but it is worth trying out a few options to see where you are most productive. Some authors insist on having a dedicated writing space – the American poet Maya Angelou even went as far as renting out her own hotel room where she could sit and focus on writing.[4] Others prefer to be among the hustle and bustle of everyday life – J.K. Rowling famously penned the *Harry Potter* series in her local café with her young daughter in tow.[5] Regardless of where you find yourself, it can be useful to associate a certain place with writing as it can help you slip more easily into a creative mindset.

Here are a few things to consider:

- **In the Home**: Is it more convenient to write in your own home? Think about where you find yourself getting into the flow the easiest? Perhaps it's a study, a corner of the kitchen, the lounge or even your garden.
- **Out and About**: If you prefer to write in different places, think about which ones best suit your needs. Do you prefer the busy atmosphere of a café or do you lean more towards the relative quiet of your local library?
- **Fitting Around Your Life**: Do you find yourself with pockets of time during the day that could provide productive writing sessions? You could consider making the most of your lunch break or daily commute, or try getting up earlier to cram in some writing time before heading out. Alternatively, you could schedule in specific writing sessions in your weekly diary if you prefer a more structured approach.
- **Be Physically Comfortable**: It is good practice to make sure you are as comfortable as possible before you start writing. It can be very distracting if you find yourself too hot or cold or sat in an uncomfortable chair.
- **Ambience**: Some authors find listening to music while writing helps get them in the zone. You could try instrumental music if you find listening to lyrics is too distracting. Likewise, are you motivated by engaging all

---

[4] Julie Zeveloff, 'Maya Angelou Always Rented A Hotel Room Just for Writing,' *Business Insider*, 28 May 2014, www.businessinsider.com/maya-angelou-writing-process-2014-5?r=US&IR=T

[5] Amy Lewis, 'Grab a coffee, write a book: The UK's most inspiring literary cafes,' *Stylist*, 2016, www.stylist.co.uk/books/grab-a-coffee-write-a-book-the-uk-s-most-inspiring-literary-cafes/127899

your senses? If so, try lighting a scented candle or having a drink that you associate with writing (caffeine seems to be the go-to choice for most authors!)

Hone Your Craft

Every writer, no matter where they are on their publishing journey, always has more to learn and that can be hugely motivational to authors seeking to write the best book they can. The great news is there are countless ways to continue developing your own writing style and improve upon your previous work.

Here are just a few ideas to get your creative juices flowing:

- **Writing Books and Articles**: There is a huge range of books and online articles on all aspects of writing, from getting started to specific areas, such as worldbuilding or characterisation.
- **Podcasts and Videos**: If you prefer to listen to or watch advice, you could also check out dedicated writing podcasts or author YouTube channels.
- **Enter Competitions or Join Writing Challenges**: Practice makes perfect, right? Or at least better than you were before. Stretching yourself by trying out competitions, challenges or creative writing prompts could be an ideal way to practice your writing, be inspired by new ideas and help you grow and learn as an author.
- **Writing Tools**: A quick online search for 'writing motivation tools' will yield thousands of results for you to explore at your leisure, from game-based apps and motivational quotes to more practical resources, such as online editing apps with inbuilt wordcount trackers.
- **Writing Classes, Workshops and Literary Festivals**: You may benefit from the learning opportunities that come from networking with other writers or be encouraged by gaining a deeper insight into the nuances of plot, structure, character development and dialogue.
- **Read**: As an aspiring author you can never read too many books. Pay attention to the storytelling devices used, how characters are developed and how the plot unfolds. You can learn a lot from reading books outside your genre in order to gain a better understanding of various writing techniques and use of language.

> **Top Tip**: Establishing a strong support network can be incredibly valuable for aspiring authors. Being accountable to others and having people cheer you on when you feel demotivated can make all the difference. Check out the 'Writing Community' chapter later in this book for a more in-depth discussion of how to find like-minded writers and the benefits that come from developing those relationships.

© July Milks/Shutterstock.com © Paul Craft/Shutterstock.com

Step Away from Your Desk

The best ideas have a tendency to arrive when you are engaged in an activity other than writing. Multitasking during more mundane tasks gives you the opportunity to mull over details such as your characters' backstories and brainstorm plot twists. There is a reason that Agatha Christie claimed the best time to plan a novel was while washing the dishes.[6]

Here are some ideas you could try out:

- **Take a bath or have a shower**: Something about being immersed in hot water always has a tendency to get the ideas flowing.

---

[6] Michael Naughton, 'Agatha Christie and the Mystery of Mindfulness,' *Michael P. Naughton*, 6 December 2015, www.michaelpnaughton.com/agatha-christie-and-the-mystery-of-mindfulness

- **Go for a walk or run**: Pumping your body full of feel-good endorphins from exercise can only be a good thing. Numerous authors endorse this method – Charles Dickens was a prolific walker, as was the poet William Wordsworth.[7]
- **Do a different hobby**: Writing can occasionally seem to take over your life, which can manifest itself as a feeling of being overwhelmed or unmotivated to continue. Spending some time enjoying another hobby, or simply having some quality time with your family and friends, can help you recapture the passion for why you started writing in the first place.
- **Take a Break**: Writing targets are important, but not if it becomes a daily drudgery. Take a break if you need to avoid burnout. Self-care is important and inevitably you'll come back feeling more energised and refreshed.

A Final Word of Encouragement

If someone hasn't told you lately, then let me be the first to say it – **what you are doing matters**. It's important. It has meaning, purpose, value and worth. If you are feeling inadequate or inferior, go ahead and stop. Just *stop*. Quiet the voice in your head and remind yourself of who you are and the convictions that have driven you to the place you currently find yourself. Then forge ahead, even when things are slow, even when things don't come easy, even when obstacles seem to place themselves in your path day after day. In the words of Harriet Beecher Stowe, 'Never give up then, for that is just the place and time when the tide will turn.'[8]

I believe in you, and so do the countless other lives who have yet to be impacted by the visions in your mind and the words at your fingertips. Tomorrow, the sun will rise and you must be ready to pursue the horizon. Wake up, rise up and let's chase it together!

---

[7] Linda Wasmer Andrews, 'To Become a Better Writer, Be a Frequent Walker,' *Psychology Today*, 28 March 2016, www.psychologytoday.com/us/blog/minding-the-body/201603/become-better-writer-be-frequent-walker

[8] Prof. Dr. Sayed Atalla, 'Never give up, for that is just the place and time that tide will turn,' *LinkedIn*, 19 January 2016, www.linkedin.com/pulse/biography-harriet-beechr-stowe-across-her-stowe-changing-atalla

About the Author
Stephen McClellan

Stephen McClellan is a Young Adult and Children's Picture Books author, an educator and an advocate. The vision behind his writing? To use the royalties earned from his books to fund local and global humanitarian projects. The proceeds from his debut Christian Fiction novel, *To Dance*, are being reinvested to support the organisation Compassion First and their fight to end sex trafficking in Southeast Asia.

The proceeds from his soon to be released debut children's picture book, *The Bat and the Mule*, will be reinvested to support the OVI Healthcare Children's Hospital in Kenya, which rescues orphans who are dying of life-threatening illnesses and diseases and nurses them back to health.

Along with writing, his passions for travel and global ministry have taken him to eleven countries on four continents to mentor youth on how to live life with purpose and intentionality. If he isn't reading, writing, or travelling, Stephen is most likely watching *The Office* or eating a bowl of mint chocolate chip ice cream. Stephen and his wife, Megan, currently live in Tennessee in the United States.

Connect Online
- **Website**: www.stephenmcclellanbooks.com
- **Facebook**: www.facebook.com/smcclellanbooks
- **Instagram**: @stephenmcclellanbooks

Plot Structure
by Kara S. Weaver

Where It All Begins

If you're a writer, chances are you're also a reader. In fact, reading may have inspired you to one day write and publish a book. Perhaps you were inspired by a dream, something you saw on your way home, the lyrics of your favourite band or a line in a book. Whatever your reason for writing, there is one important thing that you'll have to deal with and that's your **plot**. As I'm assuming you've been writing, reading and watching films for a while, I won't go into detail about what a plot is. I guess you know. But how do you create a plot that is strong, gripping and compelling enough that readers will buy your next book?

Plotting vs. Pantsing

Before I get to the point where I talk about that compelling plot, I want to make you aware of two types of writers, namely the *plotter* and the *pantser*.

A plotter is generally someone who plans everything – or almost everything – for their novel before they start writing. They flesh out the characters, write down the details of the world, pen down what happens per chapter, possibly even draw a map. A lot of plotters swear by planning ahead and using the three-act structure and beat sheets to outline their novel.

A pantser, on the other hand, is someone who sits down and writes. They have a general idea, a possible ending in mind, perhaps some scenes in between but that's it. They don't really care about three-act structures or beat sheets. They'd rather get lost in their book and see where they end up.

And then there's the **plantser, a hybrid of the aforementioned two**. They may jot down ideas in a notebook, structure their beginning, middle and ending, perhaps write down what happens in chapters in bullet points and then they get their coffee (or tea) and start writing.

Things to Be Aware of When You're a Plotter

Being a plotter means you have thought of almost everything and you know where your characters are going, what they're doing, how they're going to end up and how they can fix their problems. You might think it's easy to write the book because you've written everything down after all. One thing I've learned from my plotter friends is that it can also be a downfall to have everything written down like that, because they find it hard to let go of what they planned and release their imagination. Sometimes, it's important to go with the flow and let your characters do what *they* have planned.

Things to Be Aware of When You're a Pantser

While just sitting down and writing might sound like the best thing ever, the life of a pantser can be hard. Because you don't have a clear idea of where to go with your story, it's easy to get lost in what you're writing and put everything to paper that comes to mind. In fact, it's entirely too possible that your characters run away with you and you lose the plot. When you're aware of the fact this may happen, it's easy enough to deal with.

Whatever type of writer you are, it's important to remember none of them are wrong. Whether you're a plotter, a pantser, or a hybrid, if it works for you, go for it and stick to it. Perhaps you've even found a fourth form I'm not aware of. But whatever you are, the importance of your plot structure remains the same. If it has holes the size of the Atlantic Ocean, you'd better have a ship, because you're going to have to fix them.

> **Top Tip**: If you are a pantser, I suggest having a dedicated notebook for the story you're working on, whether on paper or on your computer, and write down key details, such as characters' appearances, quirks and habits, names of places, dates, relations, made up words and such. Trust me, it will be easier to flip through your notebook to find the information than through a finished manuscript.

Plot vs. Characters

Every book you've ever read, every film you've ever seen, every show you've ever watched, all have one thing in common: *plot*. **It's the storyline** that characters follow to get from point **A** to point **B**, whether this is straightforward or by going through the alphabet backwards to get to where they need to be. The more surprises and mysteries thrown in, the more drawn in we are. However, it's not just the plot that drives a story. Characters are equally important. In writing, there is a distinction between the two following kinds of story structures.

Plot-driven vs. Character-driven

In a plot-driven story, the action comes from a well-thought out plot. It will have rounded, intriguing characters, but in these kinds of stories, plot and structure come before deep character development as opposed to character-driven stories in which their development drives the story forward and plot and structure take a backseat.

A great example of a plot-driven story is *The Lord of the Rings* by J.R.R. Tolkien. While character development and worldbuilding is clearly important, the story is largely propelled forward by all the plot twists and turns as the hobbits set out on the mission Gandalf the wizard has bestowed upon them. Although we see how Frodo changes due to carrying the ring and how it affects those around him (Boromir, anyone?), the story would still, for the most part, continue in the same fashion had Frodo not gotten the ring, but say Aragorn. Details might change, but the ring would still have to be destroyed, so the storyline would follow the same path.

Character-driven stories are often based on real life events. Take, for example, *Memoirs of a Geisha* by Arthur Golden in which we follow the life of Chiyo/Sayuri as she is sold into servitude and is set on the path of becoming a Geisha. Almost everything that unfolds happens because of the choices she makes. When she decides to run away with her sister, and fails because she falls off the roof, her chances of ever becoming a Geisha are shattered. Although not everything happens because of her choices, but rather those of others, it's still a plot that is driven by emotion rather than complex plot twists.

With this too, whatever you choose, both approaches are fine to use. The important thing to consider is the message of your book and the best way to bring it across to your reader.

© rook76/Shutterstock.com

Writing Your Novel

Starting Your First Draft

Here's a little tip from someone who frequently fears the dreaded white page. Your first draft isn't going to be perfect. Your second draft likely won't be either. Start writing, let the words flow and don't be bothered with repetitive words and sentences just yet. All of that is for the next phase, the next draft. The most important part is that you start writing.

After I finished my first draft of my debut novel, *Crown of Conspiracy*, I pretty much discarded it and wrote a completely new second draft. That first draft had served to get out the story idea, but it was the second draft that formed the base of the story. I began rewriting my second novel, *Dance of Despair*, three times. It was the third draft I finished and built upon. This can be the downside of being a pantser, but it worked for me and although the process was strenuous and lengthy, it also gave me valuable insight into my characters and plot, but more on that later.

The Opening Line/Chapter

Whether you are a plotter, a pantser or a hybrid, we all start at the same place – an empty sheet in front of us. Wherever you look online, everybody agrees on the same thing: the most important part of your book is your opening sentence. After all, when else are you going to reel in your readers if not then? Some will forgive you if the opening line doesn't immediately draw them in as long as the first chapter does.

As a reader, what I enjoy most is when we get to know the main character while they are doing something. It can be something small or something big, as long as it gives me an idea who this character is, where they are, what they are doing, etc. If I get invested in a character early on, chances are I will finish that book with ease. When you start writing, think of the books that really captured your attention when you started. Take a few books out of your bookcase, preferably books within your genre if you have those, and have a look at what other authors did. Heck, take books out of other genres and see what you can apply to your own.

If you're still not sure about how to start, don't get stuck on it. You can keep rewriting until you're satisfied.

The Three-act Structure vs. the Plot Mountain

A lot of novels are written according to the three-act structure.[9] Research tells me this wasn't originally created for storytelling, but it was rather found that those novels that were considered to be great use this structure.

The **three-act structure** basically looks like this:

- **Act one**: the setup
- **Act two**: the confrontation
- **Act three**: the resolution

What this structure looks like in practice will be explored shortly, alongside the alternative plot mountain approach.

The **plot mountain**[10] is another structure that can be used to set up your plot. It's got a few extra steps to take, but it will give you a clear idea of the important elements.

---

[9] 'Three Act Structure: How to Nail This Story Structure in 3 Steps,' *Daily Writing Tips*, accessed 17 September 2020, www.dailywritingtips.com/three-act-structure

[10] 'Plot Mountain Definitions,' *Seneca Valley School District*, accessed 17 September 2020, www.svsd.net/cms/lib5/PA01001234/Centricity/Domain/725/PlotMountain15-16%20with%20definitions.pdf

It looks something like this:

- **Exposition**: The start of the story where characters and setting are introduced.
- **Inciting Incident**: The events of the story become complicated and conflict is shown.
- **Conflict**: The struggle between the opposing forces (internal and external).
- **Rising Action**: Events unfold and the conflict increases.
- **Climax**: Turning point for your characters. The top of intensity.
- **Falling Action**: Action after the climax. May be used or foregone.
- **Resolution**: Events following the climax. Should be short and quick. Solves the problem in the story.
- **Denouement**: Wrapping up the story and answering questions. Doesn't always occur.

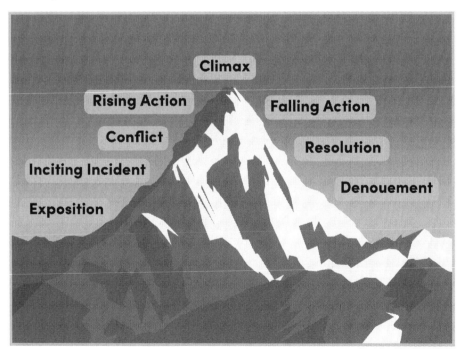

No matter what kind of writer you are, it's important to have at least a basic understanding of these structures. If you are a plotter, these structures can help you outline your story according to these steps. If you are a pantser or a hybrid, having knowledge of them may just help you streamline your story. They are used interchangeably; one cannot be used without the other. To give you a better idea what comes where, I have given each step of the two structures a short explanation below.

Act One: The Setup

In this step, you introduce your main character(s), give the reader an insight into their daily life activities and set up the *inciting incident* to kick off the *conflict*. In the plot mountain structure, this would be considered the *exposition*. This isn't just the first chapter, obviously. It's as short or long as you want to make it, but keep in mind that you don't lose your pacing and avoid the temptation to infodump and overwhelm your readers with unnecessary details. This is also where you may start the *rising action*, letting it flow over into your second act.

Act Two: The Confrontation

During this part of the story, you make life as uncomfortable as possible for your main character, which is to say that you create *conflict* they have to resolve. How they do that is up to you. Often the second part, or the middle, can become long and tedious, so now more than ever, it's important that you keep a steady pace and keep the adrenaline pumping in your readers, so to speak. Whether you write romance, crime, fantasy, sci-fi or something else, this goes for every genre.

Tying in the plot mountain, this is where the rising action flows into the *climax*, the turning point in your story for your characters. Whatever happens next, their lives have been changed and they have to figure it out somehow. At this point, the reader has become comfortable and familiar with your characters. Now is the time to make them uncomfortable.

Act Three: The Resolution

Contrary to its name, this isn't the actual resolution. This is the part where the events leading up to the *climax* and the climax itself are located. After that, you get the events following the climax. This usually isn't more than one or two chapters. In the plot mountain, this is where we would find the *falling action*, the *resolution* and, if you choose to use it, the *denouement*.

Plotting Out a Series

Whether you are writing a standalone novel or a series, the practice of plotting remains largely the same. You need to have a beginning, a middle and an end. However, the difference is that while in a standalone novel the conflict has to be resolved by the end of the book, in a series you can choose to leave the major conflict for the last book in the series.

To come back to *The Lord of the Rings* by J.R.R. Tolkien, we know the major conflict that needs to be resolved is destroying the ring, but still each book in the series has their own conflict and end goal. In the first book, *The Fellowship of the Ring*, Frodo is confronted with the ring and he agrees to meet Gandalf in Bree. When the wizard doesn't show up and Frodo has to make his own decisions, he's hurtled into problem after problem which he and his companions have to solve. Their main objective has become to bring the ring to Rivendell. Once they have, the fellowship is formed and that is when the 'bigger picture' plot is revealed; bring the ring to Mordor.

One could argue you must outline when you decide to write a series, but I can tell you from my experience as a pantser this isn't a must. What *is* important if you decide to do it without outlining the full plot is writing down important aspects of your worldbuilding, characters and sub plots. Knowing your end game could come in handy because it makes the writing process a lot easier.

The things you want to look out for when writing a series, whether you outline it beforehand or during the writing process, are as follows:

- Each book must have a beginning, a middle and an end (or the three-act structure, whatever you choose).
- The plot in each book must propel your characters further towards the main conflict and its resolution.
- If you begin something in one book but don't finish it then, make sure you conclude it somewhere in the series. When or where that happens is up to you, but each story arc and character arc must at some point be resolved.
- Work towards resolving the major conflict in each book. It doesn't always have to pan out well. In fact, it can go horribly wrong, but work towards it.

Keep in mind when writing what your publishing goals are. As an indie author, you have a lot more freedom than when you want to query in the hope of becoming traditionally published. In case of the latter, make sure you read up on what the traditional publishing standards are and how to format your manuscript and synopsis accordingly. If you are lucky enough to secure a literary agent, then you may find that they find it easier to sell a series of books to a publisher. However, that can be a huge commitment from a writing perspective, so it is important to be sure that is definitely what you want.

Compelling, Gripping Plot

Think of the books, films or series that grabbed your attention and kept it throughout. What made you go back to reading that book? What kept you watching that series? What points in the film made you sit on the edge of your seat? Then think of the books, films and series that didn't grab your attention and try to figure out what you *didn't* like about them.

In some cases, this may simply boil down to taste. In others, it may very well be that the characters had no depth, or the plot was predictable or had so many holes it would make a fishing net jealous. We humans love conflict when we can read about it or watch it (being exposed to it ourselves is quite another thing). We love to see characters struggle, fight, get kicked down and get back up. Ultimately, we want them to overcome whatever is holding them back.

A compelling, gripping plot is as much about there being enough challenging conflict as it is about the characters and their development. Don't make it easy for your characters. Don't let them win all the time. Make them struggle, make them fail, make them wish for things they cannot have, make them *want* something and take it away. Show what your characters are made of. Show your readers their fears, their desires, their quirks and their strange little habits. Make them human, even if they're not.

There is no set way to creating such characters. Some people plan them out completely, others start with a vague idea and get to know their characters as they go. And that's fine. Go for whatever works for you. Just keep in mind that you want them to be as relatable as possible. And this is not just for your protagonists but for your antagonists and your villains as well. One question that somehow works for me is a simple, 'Why do they do what they do?'

Last but Not Least

Don't forget that writing is subjective. You may have written the most compelling plot in the history of mankind, but there will still be people who won't like it. One thing I learned while writing my series is to keep within the expectations of my genre. So if you write romance, make sure you have a Happily Ever After.

Does this mean you can't experiment? That depends on your publishing goals. If you decide to go indie, feel free to experiment, but keep in mind it might not work, so be careful not to alienate your readers. If you're planning on trying the traditional route, stick to their guidelines as much as you can but don't be afraid to try something different. After all, publishers will be looking for that one book that stands out amongst so many others.

Last but not least, whichever route you choose to take, enjoy it as much as you can. Of course, there will be moments of crippling self-doubt that may send you running for the hills, but here's the thing; all authors have that. Don't compare yourself to other authors. Engage with them, learn from them, but do not ever compare yourself with them. And for those of you who struggle with perfectionism as much as I have, remember what Jodi Picoult said: 'You might not write well every day, but you can always edit a bad page. You can't edit a blank page.'[11] Keep writing because your story has an audience too. You will be someone's favourite author someday.

---

[11] Noah Charney, 'Jodi Picoult on Writing, Publishing, and What She's Reading,' *Daily Beast*, Published 3 April 2012, Updated 13 July 2017

About the Author
Kara S. Weaver

Kara S. Weaver currently lives in the Netherlands with her husband, two children and Kita the cat. English teacher by day and aspiring author by night, Kara has always loved creating fantasy worlds and characters. Not all of them have found their way onto paper yet. Language, especially the English language, is one of her many passions.

When not teaching or writing, Kara is well versed in the mysterious ways of binge-watching Netflix and speed-reading books. Occasionally, she whips out her DSLR camera to take pictures, but those days are few and far between. Other days, she finds herself painting or diamond paint-ing, whichever tickles her fancy.

Crown of Conspiracy, Kara's debut novel, is the first in *The Ilvannian Chronicles*. Since then she has also released the second book in the series, *Dance of Despair*. A prequel, *Song of Shadows*, is available as a free download from her website.

Connect Online
- **Website**: www.karasweaver.com
- **Instagram**: @kara_s_weaver

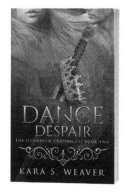

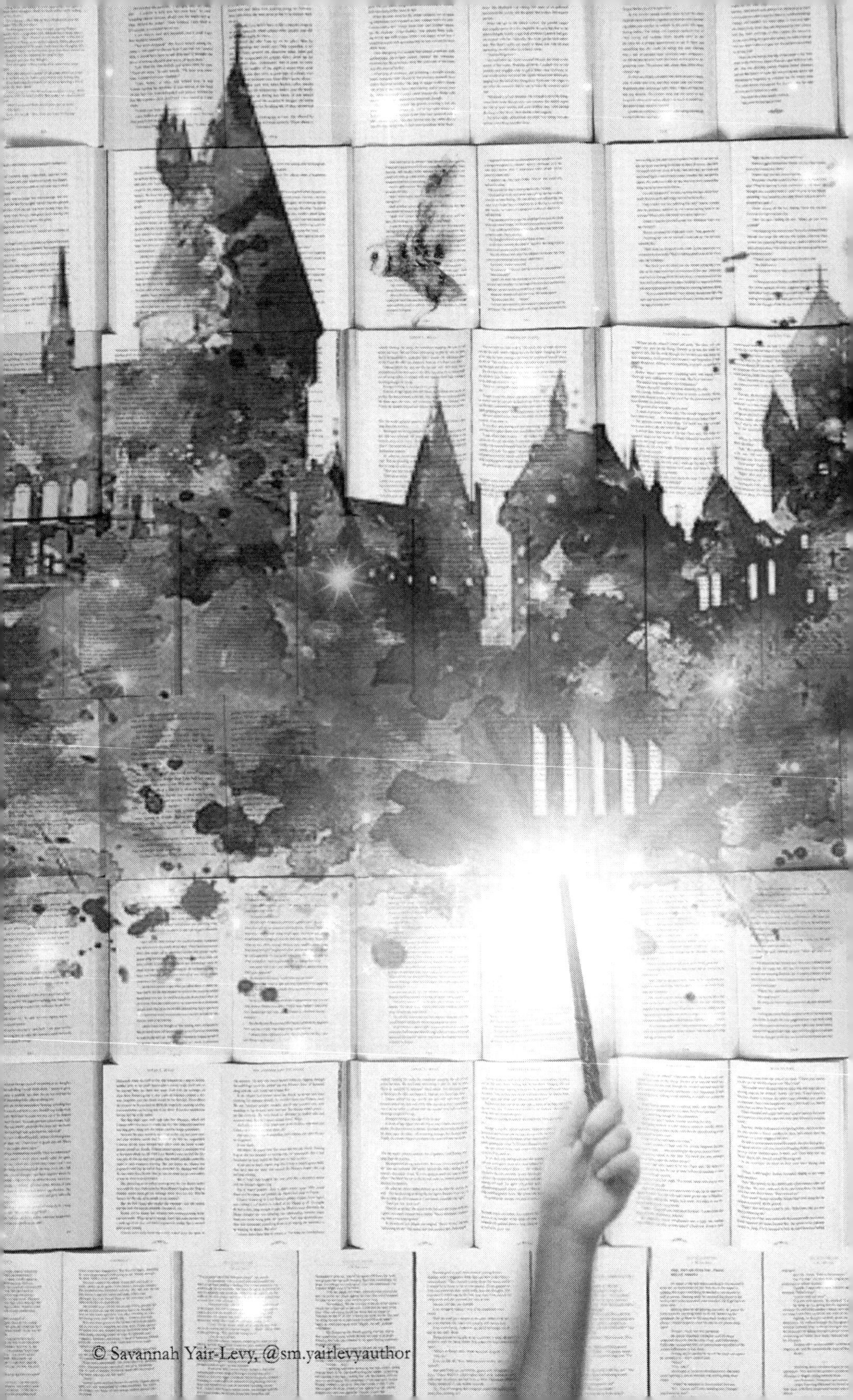

Worldbuilding
by Angeline Trevena

Building Your World

When writers think about worldbuilding, they probably summon up thoughts of Middle Earth or Narnia. They generally think about epic fantasy and big, thick books several hundred pages long. But worldbuilding can actually happen on a much smaller scale. Even a micro-scale.

While fantasy and science fiction authors may be doing the heavy lifting when creating their fictional worlds, worldbuilding exists in pretty much every genre to a certain extent. Whether it's the creation of a fictional café in a real town or imagining an alternative outcome to an event from history, any book, of any kind, can involve worldbuilding.

At the fantasy, sci-fi and horror end of the scale, the worldbuilding-heavyweights, it may mean the creation of a magic system, or monsters, to slot alongside the real world. Or it may mean building an entirely new world with new species and cultures, right up to an entire universe of planets. It can become quite the epic task!

That being said, worldbuilding doesn't need to be difficult or complicated. It doesn't need to take forever or be an excuse for never actually writing the book. It doesn't need to be overwhelming or intimidating. However, at the other end of the scale, it shouldn't be something that you haphazardly bolt on in a last-minute panic.

Worldbuilding should be tightly integrated with your plot and your characters. Your characters and their goals, their struggles, their journeys, that is the reason your readers show up. That's the reason they keep reading. You can have the most amazing world, but if you don't populate it with compelling, sympathetic and relatable characters, readers will simply stop turning the pages. Likewise, if you write amazing characters and put them into a flat, paper world, your readers won't want to walk along with them or explore with them.

Just as you want your readers to believe in your characters, you want them to believe in your world too. Let them smell the salt on the breeze, hear the buzzing of the insects. Let them feel the heat of the burning buildings and feel the oppression of the government. Let them walk every single step with your characters. Invite them in. And invite them to stay. Whether they want to set up home there or fight to change it.

Your worldbuilding is equally as important as your story and characters. Give your characters somewhere real to live, and give your readers somewhere real to visit. You simply can't separate these things out if you want to write the best book that you can.

So, what are you waiting for? Let's get started with the basics of worldbuilding.

Different Types of Worldbuilding

There are a few different ways to approach worldbuilding and which you choose will depend on your goals, your story and your genre.

Building a Whole New Fictional World

This is mostly used for writing fantasy and science fiction, and involves creating an entirely fictional world from scratch. Somewhere that does not, and never has, existed. It may have similarities to our world and it may have huge differences. Think along the lines of second-world fantasies penned by the likes of J.R.R. Tolkien (*The Lord of the Rings*) or C.S. Lewis (*The Chronicles of Narnia*).

A Real Place with an Alternative Past or Future

This may be taking a real existing place, London for example, and giving it an alternative or altered history. Imagine if the Great Fire of London had actually been started by dragons. How would that change the world today? Or alternatively, it may be taking a real-world place and throwing it into your imagined future. This is very common in dystopia, imagining an unpleasant future for our world, ironically often as an unintended consequence of attempting to create a utopia.

When using this style of worldbuilding, your map is usually, largely, already done for you. There will likely be some changes, such as missing landmarks or different names for places. The extent of the changes would entirely depend on your story and how different you have imagined the past or future of this place.

A Real Place with a Parallel Fictional World

The other approach is to set your story in a real place and have a fictional world created alongside it, usually invisible or hidden from the general public. Examples of this approach would be Neil Gaiman's *Neverwhere*, J.K. Rowling's *Harry Potter* and Mike Mignola's *Hellboy*. The fictional side of the world may be tightly integrated with the real world, or it may be quite separate. This would depend, again, on your story.

Whichever kind of world you're building, your objective is still the same: to create a believable world that your readers can really imagine walking around in.

© Mimma Key, HiddenCatch/Shutterstock.com

Map Making

One of my favourite parts of worldbuilding is making the map. You don't need to be an amazing artist; a child-like scrawl on the back of an envelope is good enough, as long as it makes sense to you so that you don't end up getting lost in your own world. Which, believe me, is surprisingly easy.

Imagine your characters are travelling from A to B. If, in one chapter, B lies west of A, and then suddenly it's south, your readers will notice. Or if B is a coastal town one minute, and a village in the mountains the next, your readers will pick up on this and it will drag them out of your story. Plus, they will love calling you out on your mistakes. They'll email you. They'll message you on social media. And they'll write it in their reviews.

As an author, your job is to keep your readers in the story. To keep them believing that it's real. To blur out their real world, their real life, and construct a new one for them for as long as they're reading your book. Glaring inaccuracies will pluck them out of your world. Inaccuracies break the illusion and remind them that they are simply reading a story. That they're not a hero fighting against a terrible foe. It pulls them back to their own cold, harsh, boring reality. And no one wants that!

And so, at the writing stage, your world map is just for you. If you're not confident in your artistic abilities, there are plenty of artists who can create a stunning map to go into the front of your book if you choose to include this later. At the early stage, the map is only for your eyes. Build it out of Lego, build it in Minecraft, mould it from clay, or cake, or whatever. As long as it's useful to you (and you're not tempted to eat it!)

And don't fall into the trap of simply drawing a map and then randomly scattering towns across it. That doesn't happen, it's not believable. Towns are founded in specific places for specific reasons. The main reason being, of course, survival.

So, imagine you're choosing a place to establish a town. What do you need? What considerations do you need to make?

Consider some of the following to get your creative juices flowing:

- **Fresh water source**. The most important and first consideration. Have you ever noticed how many major cities have a river flowing through them?
- **Varied food sources**. Man cannot live by bread alone. Or cake, sadly. Their food sources need to be varied enough to keep them healthy.
- **Natural resources**. Your characters need enough resources to be able to build their homes and the things they need. They can also use these resources for trade.
- **Appropriate land for crops and animals**. The landscape they choose to settle in will hugely impact the kind of food and animals they farm.
- **Access and security**. Can they get in and out of their settlement easily while still keeping it protected from intruders?
- **Trade route**. Can traders visit their settlement? Is it on a major trade route or will they have to rely on people making a special trip?
- **Predators**. What lives in the woods? Or the mountains? How do people protect themselves against them?

People, by and large, will choose the easiest option for their home, unless the benefits outweigh the dangers or struggles. For example, you might consider it foolish to establish a town in the middle of a dragon breeding ground. But what if just one dragon scale (which could be naturally shed) would sell for a price that could feed a family for three months. Then, it may well be worth it.

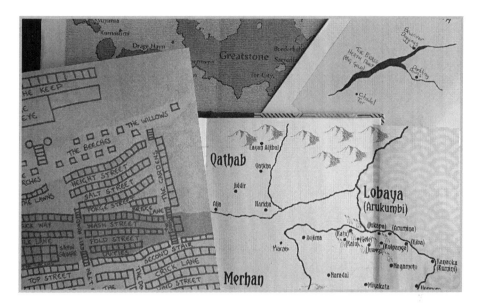

Naming Places

There are several different ways to name the places on your map. Remember that it's not just towns and cities you need to name. Depending on how big your map is, you might also be naming mountain ranges, rivers, forests, counties, countries, oceans, continents or even planets.

Just like places on your map shouldn't be randomly placed, neither should they be randomly named. They might be named after their founder, the landscape, the natural resources, the wildlife, the river or mountain they are close to. They might be named after a local legend; your place names can actually conjure up stories of their own.

Of course, you can backward engineer these things. You can find the name for a place and then create the reason it was named that. Perhaps no one remembers. Perhaps it doesn't matter to you, or your characters, or your story. As I'll discuss in the next section, you don't need a full and complete history for everything.

Top Tip: There are many online naming generators if you need some inspiration. Simply do a search and you'll find countless. I have two that I favour:

- www.squid.org/rpg-random-generator
- www.seventhsanctum.com

History

Your world is a product of everything that ever happened there, even if no one in your world still remembers. It's your job, as the writer, to know. To remember what they can't.

I'm not saying you need to plot out 5 million years' worth of history. Unless you're into that. Some people are. But you definitely need to know enough to understand why things are the way they are. To know enough to effectively create the world, its culture and values.

As people, we act according to our culture. And each culture is different. And there are variations in that culture. The things we value. The things we see as rude, or polite or unnecessary. The things we want, the things we avoid. Religion. Festivals. The way we treat our elderly or our children. The kind of food we eat and the way in which we eat it. The kind of jobs we do. The differences between rich and poor. The contrast between upper class and lower class.

And these things change over time. Invading cultures. Migrating cultures. Important events. A war or a natural disaster can hugely affect a place's culture. Changing what's important to them and the way they live their lives.

And you need to remember that every time something changes, it affects everything else.

There are different levels at which an event can occur:

- **International events**. Something that affects the entire world. Like climate change, population explosion, the sun dying or a zombie apocalypse.
- **National events**. Something that affects the country or a large area. Like an economic crash, a natural disaster or the death of a monarch.
- **Local events**. Something that affects a town or community. Such as

harvest failure, flood, a local election, the introduction of a new predator or a new trade deal.

- **Individual events**. Something that affects one person or a family. This could be a bereavement, loss of employment, loss of home, a birth, marriage or a lottery win.

It's obvious how an international event affects everything else. I'm sure a worldwide zombie outbreak would affect you and your family. But what about the other way round?

So, imagine a family preparing for a wedding. They order a whole load of wine from the next village. That gives the vineyard farmer enough money to finally leave town and live out his dream of buying a boat and exploring the seas. When the winter rain comes, the lack of the vineyard on the hillside causes a landslip which demolishes the mining town below, leading to a shortage of minerals, which leads to a shortage of coins that results in an economic crash. This is, of course, a somewhat extreme example, but it's an important thing to bear in mind. Think about the butterfly effect and the ripples you might be sending out.

Imagine your world as a pool. Every event, every construct, everything you change or create, is like dropping a pebble into the water. Sometimes, the ripples last a few minutes. Sometimes, a few years. Spreading wider. Affecting more people. Sometimes, those ripples last for centuries.

How Your World Affects Character and Story

You can also use your worldbuilding to create conflict. Remember that conflict is created when your protagonist's goal is interrupted, or opposed, and you can use your world to do that.

Perhaps the most obvious example is if the protagonist's goal requires them to break the law. But you can use other things too such as limitations of magic, social norms and expectations, or gender roles. The landscape itself can become a physical barrier, as can the weather or a lack of resources. And you can use all of this in your worldbuilding to raise the stakes and increase the tension.

Because your world doesn't exist separately from the people who live in it and you should create it with those people in mind. They will have opinions about everything. Beliefs, hopes, grievances. Things they love, things they hate. Things they want to change. Things they fight to change.

And these things will differ based on all of their nuances such as gender, age, class and religion. So their opinions will be different to the person standing next to them. They may even directly oppose one another. All of which creates conflict.

Ultimately everything comes back to character. You have to remember that you aren't writing a story about a world that happens to have people living in it. You are writing a story about people who happen to live in a particular world. *Worldbuilding. Story. Characters.* None of these are independent from each other.

Above all, *enjoy* your worldbuilding. Enjoy exploring it and watching it come to life around you. As a simple human, this may be the closest you'll come to performing real magic. To visualise an entire world from nothing. To pluck things from the air and make them real. To take breath on the wind and form it into something tangible. That is the most real, purest magic I know of.

About the Author
Angeline Trevena

Angeline Trevena was born and bred in a rural corner of Devon, but now lives among the breweries and canals of central England with her husband, their two sons and a rather neurotic cat. She is a dystopian urban fantasy and post-apocalyptic author, a podcaster and events manager.

Some years ago, she worked at an antique auction house and religiously checked every wardrobe that came in to see if Narnia was in the back of it. She's still not given up looking for it.

Angeline has published three worldbuilding guides for authors: *30 Days of Worldbuilding*, a step-by-step worldbuilding guide, *How to Destroy the World*; a guide to writing dystopia and post-apocalypse and *From Sanctity to Sorcery*; for creating religions and magic systems.

Angeline has also written a wide collection of fiction books, including *The Memory Trader* series, *The Paper Duchess* series, the *Poisonmarch* series and one standalone novel; *The Notary of Gotliss Street*. Her debut novella, *Cutting the Bloodline*, was published in 2015, and her short stories have appeared in several anthologies and magazines.

Connect Online
- **Website**: www.angelinetrevena.co.uk
- **Facebook**: www.facebook.com/angelinetrevena
- **Instagram**: @angelineandtheworld

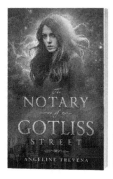

Sea of Gears and Steam

D.E. NIGHT — THE CROWNS of CROSWALD

RACHEL LANGLEY — STRU

RACHEL LANGLEY — THE MARK AND T

ANSFERENCE

Coin Toss

B.T. KEATON

Rook

I KNOW BETTER THAN TO BE AFRAID OF STORIES

Characterisation
by Tempeste Blake

Unforgettable Characters

As writers we are often juggling multiple goals as we craft a story. We want a plot that keeps the reader intrigued and eager to turn the page. We want our writing to be captivating yet invisible, lyrical yet succinct. We want to sweep the reader away.

But, no matter how much a reader loves a story, odds are they won't remember a turn of phrase, no matter how compelling. They may not recall the specific plot twist that had them applauding or throwing the book at the wall. Readers may become engrossed in the world the author built and enjoy every moment, but later not be able to rattle off a single detail.

A multi-dimensional, unique character, however, one that connects readers to the plot, the world, and the story…they are unforgettable.

Emma Woodhouse. Sherlock Holmes. Daisy Buchanan. Mr. Darcy. These complex characters stay with us long after we finish the book, sometimes for the rest of our lives, even when we have forgotten specifics of the plot. Their character development is so well done, we often think of them as real people.

© Ostill is Franck Camhi/Shutterstock.com

Defining Character Development

Character development can be defined as:[12]

- 1. **The process by which an author develops a detailed character profile**. This activity is usually done in conjunction with plot development and takes place as part of the planning process, before the writer actually starts to write.
- 2. **Character development also refers to the way a character changes through the course of the novel**, generally in response to the experiences and events gathered through the course of the story itself. This is known as the character arc.

This definition not only emphasises the importance of developing fully-rounded and lifelike characters who are believable as real people, but it also references the creation of the journey the characters go on throughout the course of the story. This is worth remembering as you begin your planning (or dive straight into writing if you are more of a pantser). Your characters don't exist in isolation, their development is propelled by the plot which impacts them in some way. The combination of these two elements is what can make a character truly unforgettable.

So how do we create characters that stick with readers after they've put the story back on the shelf? Countless books have been written and entire master classes have been taught on the subject. I've devoured many of them and continue to add character creation tools to my toolbox.

Below I'll share some of my favourite tips that you may find useful as well.

Give Characters a Goal They Don't Realise They Have

Memorable characters want something to change in their lives. They need a goal that encourages the reader to follow along to see if they attain it. All the better if the thing they *think* they want is different than what they actually need.

When my daughter was a toddler, we'd watch her favourite television shows which were, of course, littered with toy advertisements. She'd break

---

[12] Harry Bingham, 'Character Development – And The Ultimate Character Bio,' *Jericho Writers*, accessed 11 August 2020, www.jerichowriters.com/hub/character

from her mesmerised trance and wiggle on the couch, pointing to the TV proclaiming, 'I want that.' But, when her birthday rolled around and one of those things happened to be wrapped up for her pleasure, she'd play with the new toy for only a short time and then return to crayons and scrap paper. What she needed to be content didn't always mesh with what she thought she wanted. Many people, myself included, are the same. Show of hands if you have a trendy gadget or outfit (or three) tucked away in a closet that you never even used. Both my hands are raised!

Our characters are no different.

In book two of my *Riley's Peak* series, *Chasing Gravity*, my character Tish Duchene *wanted* to find her missing mother and then focus on reinventing herself after leaving the military. But what she came to learn over the course of the novel was that she *needed* something she'd not been able to admit to herself; to come to terms with a trauma from her past.

As you think about your character's arc, throw in the want vs. need dilemma for them and it will add to their dimension. Remember it is the reader's understanding of these character motivations that will lead them to empathise with them and become emotionally invested in their journey.

Give Characters a Unique Voice So They Are Recognisable Without Being Named

Realistic and unforgettable characters are as unique as people are in real life. Character voice, including dialogue, internalisation and even body language all work together to add layers to the people (and beings for you sci-fi writers) you have created.

With dialogue, ideally, we want each character to have their own distinct way of verbalising. When you're away from your writing desk and out and about, make a point to listen to the voices around you. Notice speech patterns, repeated words and verbal tics. Take note of the speed at which some people speak compared to others. All these things can add vibrancy to your character's dialogue. Many years ago, I had a friend who occasionally used malapropisms without realising it. She once told someone they were an, 'Alcatraz around her neck.' She of, course meant, 'albatross.' I've never forgotten it and still smile when I think about it. One of my characters in *Chasing Symmetry*, Tucker Baranski, charmingly has the same affliction. He says 'neons' instead of 'eons,' and 'plutonic' instead of 'platonic,' making him instantly recognisable to the reader even without a dialogue tag.

Like spoken dialogue, internalisation and body language can set your characters apart. Think about how your characters self-talk and make sure they are differentiated. When this is done well, readers should be able to tell each character without being named. One character may suck her teeth when frustrated, another character may habitually count to five in their head before they speak, another may have perpetually sloped shoulders that could either indicate a lack of confidence or a bad back.

Of course, you want to use things like this sparingly, but they can make each character unique and memorable.

And you don't always have to leave the house to gather information about the way people speak, interact and carry themselves. Now more than ever in the age of social media it's easy to get a glimpse. Have a character in their teens? Hop on social media for the inside track on 'teenspeak.'

Let Your Secondary Characters Do Some of the Heavy Lifting

Sometimes I love creating secondary characters (and even tertiary characters) more than my primary characters. It's a fun challenge to give them their own life without taking away from the main characters or storyline. One of my favourite characters from my debut novel, *Chasing Symmetry*, Maris Romero, has 'a laugh that can be heard across the state' and would never be missed when she enters a room. It was often a balancing act to keep her from stealing the scene from her best friend and lead character, Bianca James, so I focused on sharing characteristics of Maris that would reveal more about Bianca and about their friendship, than about Maris on her own. That's not to say Maris isn't a fully realised character with her own wants and needs, but one of her main tasks is to drive the story forward and help add layers to who Bianca is.

Along the same lines, your antagonist, who may be fully intent on doing everything in their power to keep your protagonist from achieving their goals, can also be used to add further dimension to your main characters.

Be That Nosy Neighbour Who Drives You Nuts

You know those people, the ones who ask a million questions about where you're from, what you ate for breakfast, who your celebrity crush was in high school and is now. Guilty as charged. Though not in real life, in the real world I'm more of a listener than a talker, but I pester my characters non-stop. I've given them the Myers-Briggs personality test, written pages of backstory about them, created vision boards to build their wardrobe, house and first pet.

It is important to do your research in order to realistically flesh out your characters. Anything that goes beyond your scope of direct experience should ideally be thoroughly researched, whether that is a certain job role, the place they live or their religion, sexual orientation, disability or ethnicity.

Online research is a great starting point, as are books about these topics. But it would be even more valuable to talk to people similar to your characters if possible as they will be able to provide a much deeper insight and share their own personal experiences. This may help you to incorporate more inclusive language and weave tangible examples into your book.

Diversity in books is incredibly important, but you may want to consider using a sensitivity reader if you do not belong to the marginalised group you are writing about. Sensitivity readers assess a manuscript prior to publication and improve it by helping to eliminate stereotypes, bias, inaccuracies and false information.

Early on in my fiction writing journey, I'd hear writers talk about the characters making their own decisions. Frankly I thought that was silly. How could a fictional character decide what they'd eat for breakfast? The writer certainly would need to make that decision. The writer is the one pulling the puppet strings. But as I delved further into character development, over time, I began to see what writers meant by that. The more we get to know our characters, the more they come to life in our minds and the more they do start to make their own decisions. I've often looked back over my draft for the day and realised a character did something without me putting much thought into it. They've become so three-dimensional in my mind that my subconscious takes over. This is the real power of character creation. The more they are real to the writer, the more they leap off the page.

Top Tip: If you're interested in understanding what makes your characters tick, the Myers-Briggs personality test is freely available to use at **www.16personalities.com**. This site provides a comprehensive description of every personality type, including details about their strengths and weaknesses, romantic relationships, friendships, parenthood, career paths and workplace habits. Answer the test as your different characters and the results can be very enlightening.

Give Characters Real, Relatable Flaws

Honestly, this is sometimes a challenge for me. After living with characters for months, sometimes years, I grow protective of them. My maternal instinct kicks in and I want to protect them from mistakes. How can I let a character smoke when I know all too well how unhealthy that is? But flaws are true to life and if you try to protect your character, they start to lose dimension.

These flaws can vary in degrees among your characters. Not every character needs to be unreliable and continually making bad choices about their lives. Feel free to mix it up with your characters and let them grow and learn from each other. How one character reacts to another's mistake can be very revealing.

Additionally, don't feel like you need to keep them boxed in. By that I mean, once you've established a character trait don't feel they always need to stay in that lane. So much can be revealed by the occasional step out of their normal bounds. A chatterbox character who suddenly grows quiet around a new co-worker with a chin so chiselled it could cut glass shows the reader how she feels about this new person without the writer needing to tell. If your characters catch you, the writer, by surprise, they're sure to engage the reader as well.

Top Tip: Challenge yourself to come up with a number of both positive and negative personality traits for every character. This combination of strengths and weaknesses will help to make them more well-balanced and will prevent your protagonists becoming too idealistic and give your antagonists a morality; after all, no one ever thinks that they are a villain.

Don't Be Afraid to Draw from Real Life

My favourite coffee mug that I keep front and centre on my desk reads, 'Please do not annoy the writer, she may put you in a book and kill you.' Though I of course, protect the innocent (and not so innocent) by changing names and details, I've drawn plenty of my characters' quirks and actions from real life. As previously mentioned, with the malapropisms, I don't hesitate to let the things people say and do around me flavour my fiction. People are endlessly fascinating and surprising, so do continue to take notes and give your characters added interest by drawing from your own life experiences.

Multi-task With Physical Description

There are multiple schools of thought when it comes to a character's physical description. I've heard readers say they need the writer to give more details so they can really see the characters, and I've heard other readers say they like to make up their own visual so they can imagine themselves as that character. I tend to try to describe in a way that's somewhere in between. As mentioned above, I have stacks of character notebooks that describe every detail down to mole placement, length of fingers and true hair colour beneath the dye job, only a small portion of which makes it into the story, but it helps me to see the character in full and living colour.

The more those descriptions multi-task, the better. Working in that a character's generally perfectly styled butter-toned hair is dishevelled, shows the reader far more than simply saying her hair was the colour of butter. And don't feel that colour is always the best tool in the kit. When you describe a character's eyes as sad, you're certainly sharing far more than if you'd mentioned their baby blues. Spice it up!

Consider how your characters' personality traits can be physically expressed. For example, if someone is excited, do they bounce their knee when sitting, fidget in anticipation or have palms so sweaty they need a towel? This is an example of '**show, don't tell**,' an adage many writers learn early on in their writing endeavours. According to Reedsy, this technique 'fosters a style of writing that's more immersive for the reader, allowing them to "be in the room" with the characters.'[13]

---

[13] 'Show, Don't Tell: Tips and Examples of The Golden Rule,' *Reedsy*, 11 July 2019, https://blog.reedsy.com/show-dont-tell

I often think of Russian novelist Anton Chekhov's quote, 'Don't tell me the moon is shining; show me the glint of light on broken glass.'[14] Using this method can be effective in bringing your characters to life in a way that goes beyond simply listing their personality traits. This involves the reader in the story in a much more compelling way.

When you show the reader your character, don't feel compelled to give a full head-to-toe description the minute your character first arrives on the scene. Titbits scattered throughout the novel tend to be more effective.

Top Tip: Be mindful about which descriptions you have a tendency to overuse in your writing. For me, eyes may very well be the 'window to the soul,' but they are also my Achilles heel. When I was working through an early draft of my first novel, I used the search feature to determine how often I relied on eyes for description. Thank goodness we live in the automated, search function age because I was able to quickly assess that I was overusing eye colour and scale back.

Throw Your Characters into the Deep End

The most memorable characters don't have it easy. They battle internal and external conflict from beginning to end, and hopefully learn something along the way. One of the most widely known characters of all time, Scarlett O'Hara from *Gone with the Wind*, faces a very real battle to survive during the civil war while dealing with an internal battle between a man she thinks she loves and a man she thinks she hates. Talk about conflict!

As it relates to character, conflict can come in a variety of forms. Your characters could be battling themselves, another character, outside forces or even a supernatural force. The type of conflict doesn't matter so much. What does matter is that you show your characters facing and overcoming (or at times succumbing) to difficult situations.

Tap Into All Five Senses

One valuable way of describing your characters in a captivating fashion is to employ the use of all five senses. Obviously be careful not to go

---

[14] Krista Stevens, 'The glint of light on broken glass,' *The Daily Post*, 4 January 2015, https://wordpress.com/dailypost/2015/01/04/the-glint-of-light-on-broken-glass/

overboard as this would quickly become too distracting, but incorporating meaningful details can help readers better visualise your fictional characters, which provides a rich and immersive experience.

Sight: Helen pursed her lips in a sour pucker. She shook her head defiantly; tips of dangly mismatched earrings brushing her shoulders. One feathery. One all beads and stars.

Sound: The sing-song quality in Jewel's voice did little to mask her hostility.

Touch: Padding barefoot over to him, she relished the warmth of the wooden floorboards underfoot.

Taste: He dropped four small ice cubes into the tumbler of scotch, swirled it and took a sip. The first taste transported him away to a land of kilts, bagpipes and lazy afternoons.

Smell: He draped his forearms across the door, drawing so close she could smell salami and hot mustard on his breath.

Develop Their Feelings

When describing how characters react in different situations, go beyond the obvious and consider what specific types of emotions they are experiencing. For example, rather than simply being angry, consider if they are acting critical, aggressive or humiliated. Then go even further and explore if they are being critical because they are sceptical or dismissive. Are they acting aggressively because they are hostile or have been provoked? Do they feel humiliated due to being disrespected or ridiculed? Identifying why a character is feeling a certain emotion goes a long way in creating complex characters due to having a deeper level of understanding.

The Feelings Wheel[15] created by Dr Gloria Willcox is a fantastic resource for identifying different words to describe emotions.

If you need further inspiration, the following books are excellent:

- *The Emotion Thesaurus: A Writer's Guide to Character Expression* by Angela Ackerman and Becca Puglisi
- *The Emotional Wound Thesaurus: A Writer's Guide to Psychological Trauma* (Writers Helping Writers Series) by Angela Ackerman and Becca Puglisi

Parting Words

As mentioned there are countless resources for creating compelling characters. Classes, blog posts, books, videos, checklists and personality quizzes. As with other areas of writing there are no hard and fast rules to character development. By reading widely and studying the characters that you find intriguing, you'll be able to craft your own multi-dimensional characters that leap off the page and stay with the reader forever.

---

[15] 'The Feelings Wheel,' 1 May 2020, *Calm*, https://blog.calm.com/blog/the-feelings-wheel

About the Author
Tempeste Blake

When Nancy Smith and Cat Trizzino met in an online writers' group, their individual styles blended to a shared vision. Though they live in different states, Nancy in Michigan, Cat in Maryland, their passion for well-crafted stories makes the physical distance irrelevant.

Tempeste Blake is the result of their combined voices, an author who writes grab-the-tissue-box, heart-in-your-throat romantic suspense and loves to throw her characters into the deep end to see if they sink or swim. Tempeste is currently spending time with characters new and old as she works on the next book in her *Riley's Peak* Series.

This 'Characterisation' chapter was written by Cat Trizzino.

Connect Online
- **Website**: www.tempesteblake.com
- **Facebook**: www.facebook.com/Tempeste.Blake
- **Instagram**: @tempesteblakeauthor
- **Twitter**: @TempesteBlake

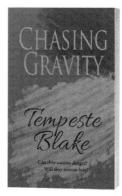

WRITE
WITHOUT
FEAR.

EDIT
WITHOUT
MERCY.

Editing
by Candice Bellows

Do I Really Need an Editor?

When I hear authors say things like, 'I don't need an editor – I've got a spellchecker' or 'I'll just use Grammarly,' I like to tell them the story of the time my editing saved the life of a knight.

As a teenager, I took a playwriting class with my younger sister, whom I'll call Julie. One day, she asked me for feedback on some of her work. In the scene in question, two knights duelled and the loser knelt to beg for mercy. It was a dramatic moment, which I promptly ruined because I started laughing.

The problem? Julie had given this line to the defeated knight: 'Please spear me.'

To date, this is the only spelling mistake I've ever encountered that completely reversed the intended meaning of a sentence!

Once I explained what was so funny, Julie and I had a good chuckle. She corrected the error, and the poor knight was ~~speared~~ spared.

But editing is much more than fixing unintentionally hilarious misspellings. It's an integral part of the publishing process – one that no author can afford to skip.

What Is Editing?

One of the biggest points of confusion about editing is what, exactly, that term means. Going strictly by the dictionary, editing is '[preparing] (something, such as literary material) for publication or public presentation.'[16] However, that preparation process is much more complicated than this definition implies.

---

[16] *Merriam-Webster*, s.v. "edit (verb)," accessed 21 July 2020, www.merriam-webster.com/dictionary/editing

In fact, editing involves reading and reviewing a manuscript multiple times with an increasingly narrow focus. These different types of examination are called *levels of editing*. Not all manuscripts need to pass through all the levels, but every manuscript should undergo at least some of them.

You should, of course, do as much self-editing as you can before you approach a professional editor (if you plan to self-publish) or contact literary agents (if you hope to be traditionally published). As the author, you need to make sure your manuscript is as polished as you can make it before handing it off to someone else. Coincidentally, this practice will likely save you a lot of money down the road. We'll talk more about self-editing later in this chapter.

For now, let's look at each of the different editing levels in more depth.

Level 1: Developmental Editing

During *developmental editing*, a developmental editor (DE) helps the author define the overall structure and content of the book. For a fiction manuscript, the author and DE focus on elements such as plot, character arcs, theme, etc. For a nonfiction manuscript, the author and DE discuss factors such as the work's thesis, structure, supporting evidence and so on. Regardless of genre, developmental editing addresses issues that affect the entire manuscript or large portions of it, such as chapter order.

Because developmental editing ripples through every part of the book, this step often takes place before or during the writing of a manuscript. In the latter case, it's sometimes known as *book coaching*. Having this support before and during writing can help authors catch potential problems early so they don't turn into larger issues later. However, developmental editing can also take place after a manuscript is complete.

Developmental editing tends to be the most expensive level of editing for two reasons. First, it typically takes more time than any other level. Second, while the publishing world has many specific rules for matters such as spelling, grammar and capitalisation, few industry guidelines exist for developmental editing. Thus, of all the types of editors, a DE relies the most heavily on his or her experience and professional judgment. This lack of formal rules is also why automated tools such as Grammarly (which have to be programmed with exact guidelines) can't help you with developmental editing. For this part of the process, you absolutely must have a human DE on your team.

Not every manuscript needs developmental editing. However, before you have any other editing done, it's always a good idea to have a DE evaluate your manuscript and confirm whether or not it would benefit from developmental editing.

Level 2: Substantive Editing

Once an author has a complete manuscript and any developmental editing is finished, *substantive editing* (sometimes called *line editing* or *content editing*) can begin. The line between developmental editing and substantive editing can be nebulous. If a DE frames the house that is your manuscript, a substantive editor (SE) sets up and tests all the plumbing, wiring and other essential systems within that house. Like DEs, SEs have to make many subjective judgment calls based on their experience, so automated tools provide little or no help with this part of the editing process.

Substantive editing examines and improves the flow of ideas within a manuscript. An SE looks for problems with logic, tone, diction (word choice), coherence (whether ideas are expressed clearly), cohesion (whether the transitions between ideas, paragraphs and sections feel smooth) and other issues that affect whole paragraphs and sentences. This level of editing might involve rearranging or even rewriting sentences or paragraphs.[17]

---

[17] 'Member Skills,' *Editorial Freelancers Association*, last modified 2020, www.the-efa.org/hiring/member-skills

If an SE begins rewriting lengthy passages, however, one of two issues may be occurring:

- The manuscript might not truly be ready for substantive editing and may need to undergo (more) developmental editing first.
- The SE is using too heavy a hand. Editors are usually trained to avoid doing this, but it can still happen.

If you find yourself in this situation, it's time to have a heart-to-heart with your SE so the two of you can determine the source of the problem and how to proceed.

As with developmental editing, not every manuscript needs substantive editing. In fact, a thorough developmental edit can greatly reduce the amount of substantive editing a manuscript needs. But again, it's always a good idea to get an SE's opinion before you decide whether or not to put your manuscript through this level of editing.

Level 3: Copyediting

After any developmental and substantive editing are finished, *copyediting* can begin. This level is what most people think of when they hear the word *editing*. It involves checking for and correcting mistakes in spelling, usage, grammar, punctuation, capitalisation, syntax, tense, etc. Every manuscript should pass through the hands of a copyeditor (CE) before publication.

Many of the rules that guide the copyediting process are codified in reference materials known as *style manuals*. Each country uses different style manuals, so choosing which manual to follow is one of the first decisions you should make for your book.

For example, in the United States, some of the most widely used style manuals include these works:

- *The Chicago Manual of Style* ('Chicago style')
- *MLA Handbook for Writers of Research Papers* ('MLA style')
- *The Associated Press Stylebook* ('AP style')
- *Publication Manual of the American Psychological Association* ('APA style')

This is what editors or publishers mean when they say things such as, 'All our books follow Chicago style' or 'We use AP style.'

Speaking of publishers, traditional publishers and some independent publishers use certain style manuals for all their books. If you are self-publishing and not using an independent publishing company, then the choice of style manual is yours. But the rules of copyediting vary considerably among different style manuals and even among different editions of the same style manual, so you absolutely must specify which manual and which edition of that manual you are using before your CE starts work.

> **Top Tip**: For matters of spelling, your CE will rely heavily on a dictionary, so make sure to clarify which dictionary and which edition of it to use. If the language in which you're writing has regional variations in spelling and usage (e.g., American English vs. British English), also identify which variation should apply to your work.

Because copyediting uses so many specific rules, it tends to be fairly straightforward, requiring fewer judgment calls than other levels of editing. Thus, it tends to be the least expensive level. Automated tools such as spellcheckers and online editing tools including Grammarly, ProWritingAid and AutoCrit can also greatly assist with and even speed up copyediting, but they still can't replace a human CE. For instance, my sister's 'spear me' mistake managed to outwit her spellchecker, and when I tested that sentence years later in the Grammarly and ProWritingAid tools, both of them failed to find anything wrong. Yikes.

What Isn't Editing?

Many writers also use certain processes that don't fall under the umbrella of editing but do provide important feedback on books. Let's look at some of those methods.

Alpha Reading

If you choose to use *alpha reading*, it takes place after you've finished a draft or two of your manuscript. A trusted person called an alpha reader reads an early draft of your book and provides feedback on whether the book 'works' overall and whether there are any major issues with it. You should have only one or two alpha readers so you don't get overwhelmed with feedback at this early stage of the project.[18]

Beta Reading

Beta readers come into the publishing process after you've done some further refining of your book. You might bring these readers on board after you've self-edited the manuscript and before you send it to your editor, or you might wait until your editor has finished with the manuscript. Regardless of the exact timing, beta readers read later drafts of your book and give you feedback on parts that aren't working. This feedback could include anything from typos to larger problems with the story.

For best results, choose beta readers with interest and experience in your genre.[19] To make your readers' feedback even more meaningful, give them a list of issues to look for and/or questions you have about the manuscript (e.g., 'Do you find Monica's motivation believable in chapter 4? Why or why not?').[20]

Proofreading

Proofreading is a final check of a manuscript for lingering errors. Unlike editing, this process fixes only things that are objectively wrong, such as misspellings or left-out punctuation. Ideally, the proofreader should be someone who has never seen the manuscript before, because familiarity can lead our brains to trick us into seeing what we know the text *should* say instead of what's actually there.

Proofreading can happen at two different points in the publishing process. Every manuscript should undergo proofreading after the designer has laid out the book and inserted all the text. Besides sweeping for typos, this proofread ensures that no text has disappeared or ended up in the wrong place. As a further safeguard against typos, you could also have the manuscript proofread earlier, before you send it to the designer.

---

[18] 'Big Al, 'The Difference between Alpha, Beta, and ARC Readers,' *Indies Unlimited*, 6 December 2016, www.indiesunlimited.com/2016/12/06/the-difference-between-alpha-beta-and-arc-readers

[19] Visit www.thewritelife.com/ultimate-guide-to-beta-readers for more information about choosing and working with beta readers.

[20] Big Al, 'The Difference.'

Who Can Help Me with Editing?

Many writers have friends or family members review their manuscripts before publication. While this can be helpful, most of these people don't have editorial training. They also might not provide needed feedback because they don't want to hurt the author's feelings. So, whom can you turn to when you need professional help with your manuscript?

If you work with a traditional publisher, in-house staff or freelancers hired by the publisher will take care of all the editing, design and proof-reading for your book. But if you choose to self-publish, you'll have to create your own team to fulfil these functions. Alpha and beta readers are typically unpaid volunteers, but for the other steps, you'll need to hire and pay independent professionals.

When you search for your team members, make sure to find the right type of person for each function you need. For example, an alpha reader can't do your substantive editing, and a proofreader can't do a developmental edit. Some providers offer multiple services, while others specialise in only one or two. To avoid wasting time and money, always double-check whether the people you choose actually provide the service(s) you're looking for. For example, if someone says he or she offers developmental editing, ask what that involves so you can make sure that you and the provider have the same expectations.

Pros and Cons of Editing

Like anything in life, professional editing has its pros and cons. Let's look at some of the most common ones.

Pro #1: Personal and Professional Growth

Working with professional editors can enhance and even accelerate your growth as a writer. It's often said that we learn more from our mistakes than we do from our successes. An editor's primary job is to point out and help a writer fix errors. With this increased awareness, you can consciously work to overcome your weaknesses and improve your writing with each project.

Pro #2: Consistency, Professionalism and Quality

One of the biggest advantages of working with professional editors is that you reap the benefits of their experience and natural gifts. Regardless of what formal training they've had, editors have both the passion and the knack for finding the best ways to use language for specific purposes. Their training, especially if they've previously worked in traditional and/or self-publishing, makes them intimately familiar with style guides, common mistakes, sensitive topics and other industry-specific knowledge that average readers simply don't have. Editors know that consistency is key and quality is everything, and they constantly have those goals in the backs of their minds as they work. They know how to deliver feedback in ways that clearly but kindly show what needs improvement – and what's working well. They work as partners, not coauthors or dictators, with writers and support their quest to create the best books possible.

Con #1: Scams

Unfortunately, not all publishing professionals live up to the *professional* part of their titles. As in any industry, some individuals and companies behave unethically. They might make false promises, try to unnecessarily rewrite clients' books, charge exorbitant (or ridiculously low) prices and do a terrible job, steal manuscripts and publish them as their own, or simply take authors' payments and disappear without doing any work. These scoundrels – who make honest editors' blood boil – are not worth your time and certainly not worth your money. So, how do you avoid them?

A provider's website can help you start the vetting process. Look for features such as client testimonials or lists of past work. These are signs that the provider has completed earlier projects and satisfied other customers. If a provider doesn't have a website at all or doesn't list any testimonials or past work, he or she might be new to the industry – or a scammer.

While on the provider's website, also look at his or her rates. The Editorial Freelancers Association (EFA), one of the most influential organisations of freelance publishing professionals, offers common rates for various levels of editing at **www.the-efa.org/rates**. If a provider charges significantly less than these rates – such as copyediting for $0.0005 (US) per word – this should raise a red flag. What seems like a bargain price may be a sign of an inexperienced or fraudulent editor.

Another useful resource for weeding out unscrupulous providers is the Alliance of Independent Authors. Its Watchdog Desk rates many publishing-services providers and notes any issues that authors have experienced with them. Of course, not every provider is on this list, but it can help you vet someone you're considering hiring. You can find the list at **www.selfpublishingadvice.org/best-self-publishing-services**.

Finally, try reaching out to your own network. If you belong to authors' groups on Facebook or other social media, ask if anyone has worked with the provider you're considering. Especially if the provider's website doesn't include any testimonials, the responses you get can be invaluable.

For example, almost a year ago, several editors in a Facebook group mentioned some unpleasant interactions they'd had with a potential client of mine. While I try not to make decisions based on hearsay, it often has some truth in it. I'd also already noticed multiple red flags about this person and his manuscript, so the Facebook discussion simply confirmed the decision I'd been leaning towards. I turned down the potential client, and he decidedly validated my choice by throwing a virtual tantrum so abusive and profane that I had to block him on email and social media. Forget dodging a bullet – I think I dodged a nuclear warhead there!

Con #2: Price

In my experience, price is always the biggest sticking point for authors seeking professional editing. There are no two ways about it: editing is expensive.

You're likely thinking, 'Well, how expensive is *expensive*?' Before we get to the specifics on pricing, let me give you some context through one of my more memorable editing experiences. This story is abridged from an email I sent to my private subscribers on March 5, 2020.

> A few years ago, when I was working for a traditional publisher, a much-anticipated manuscript turned up in my inbox. (I'm being deliberately vague about the details to protect the author's privacy.) The subject of this book was one that many readers need help with and that I was curious about, so I was eager to tackle the project.
>
> When I opened the file…oh, my goodness.
>
> First of all, the spelling, grammar and usage were among

the worst I'd ever seen. As I read, I also found that several important subtopics had insufficient support, most of the chapters needed to be split and/or reordered, the source citations were a mess and more. To top it off, the author was nervous about the publishing process and sometimes swamped both the marketing department and me with emails.

In the eighteen months I worked for that publisher, no other project took so long or required so much work. Just the various levels of editing done on that book took about six months to complete. Even factoring out the time that I had to spend on other projects during that period, that was still 700 to 800 hours' worth of work on a single manuscript. By my calculations, a manuscript with a similar wordcount and comparable editing needs would normally take – at the very worst – about 400 hours to complete.

This is an extreme example, but it powerfully illustrates how much a single book can cost. If we break down the salary I was making at the time into an hourly wage, it comes out to $21.75 (US) (far lower than the EFA's listed rates for any level of editing). This means that the editing alone – never mind the salaries of the designers and the marketing team, the benefits provided to the employees who worked on the book, or the price of the printing – cost over $15,000.

Does it now make a bit more sense why professional editing is so expensive? Instead of a traditional publisher covering all these costs and possibly giving you an advance on your royalties, you're covering all these costs yourself.

So, how high do those costs work out to be? For quality work by trained professional editors, expect to spend several thousand dollars (US) on each level of editing. I've heard of just developmental editing costing between $5,000 and $10,000. The higher the wordcount of a manuscript, the more editing it needs and the more experienced the editor, the higher the price will be. If a provider offers to edit your manuscript for rates such as $0.0005 per word, that person likely either doesn't know the value of their services or isn't doing a thorough job – both bad signs.

Now, before you run away screaming from the idea of professional editing, there are some things you can do to help lower the costs. Let's look at those next.

Ways to Lower Your Editing Costs

Method #1: Self-Editing

You know your book better than anyone. That makes you the first and possibly most important editor your manuscript will have. The more editing you do yourself, the less time and energy a professional editor will need to spend on your manuscript and, therefore, the less the editing will cost.

How Do You Self-Edit?

Many books and web articles exist to help you with self-editing, so take some time to search the internet for them and read them. You can also use those oft-mentioned automated tools – spellcheckers, Grammarly, ProWritingAid, AutoCrit and more – to help cut down on copyediting issues such as grammar, usage and spelling mistakes. Even if you're not ready for copyediting yet, a cleaner manuscript makes a DE's or SE's job quicker and easier by reducing distractions. I'll let you in on a secret: most editors learn copyediting first, and even when we're performing other levels of editing, it can be really hard to turn our CE brains off.

I also highly recommend that you create a *style sheet* as you write. This is a list of words, phrases, abbreviations and so on that get special treatment in your manuscript. For instance, you might have entries such as, 'Federal Bureau of Investigation (FBI): Spell out on first mention, abbreviate thereafter' or 'Use British spelling and punctuation conventions throughout.' When I'm writing or editing fiction, I also use the style sheet to keep track of details about characters or places so that, for instance, a half-Cajun protagonist doesn't have a Cajun father in chapter 1 but a Cajun mother in chapter 5 (a mistake I once found in a published novel).

Not only will a style sheet help you keep track of what you want in your book, but it'll also be an invaluable tool for your editors. Instead of having to contact you about every question they have, they'll often be able to find the answers and make the necessary fixes themselves by consulting the style sheet.

Top Tip: To maximise your effectiveness while self-editing, you can choose from many techniques. Some authors find it useful to read the text aloud, change the font before editing, print out the pages and edit them by hand or take a break from writing before launching into editing. Many free online checklists can also help guide you through the self-editing process. I recommend starting with *How to Edit a Book: The Ultimate Free 21-Part Checklist* by Jerry Jenkins.[21]

Method #2: Learn Your Style Guide

Another way to cut down your editing costs is to learn and follow the style guide you'll be using. This doesn't mean that you have to become a professional editor yourself! But if you memorise common rules from your style guide, such as whether or not to use serial commas or how to correctly format citations (which your editors will love you for doing, by the way), you can prevent or fix these issues yourself. Again, the less your editors have to do to your manuscript, the more money you can save.

---

[21] 'How to Edit a Book: Your Ultimate 21-Part Checklist,' *Jerry Jenkins*, accessed 31 August 2020, www.jerryjenkins.com/self-editing

Method #3: Use Alpha and/or Beta Readers

I know I said earlier that alpha and beta readers can't replace professional editors. They can't. However, because alpha and beta readers are usually volunteers, they can tell you many of the same things an editor would tell you – but for free. If a problem in your manuscript jumps out and bites an alpha or beta reader on the nose, you can bet your editors and future readers will notice it too. Then you can fix that issue yourself for free (if you have the time) or at least point it out to your editors (so they don't have to spend extra time and more of your money looking for it).

Furthermore, alpha and beta readers give you feedback from the perspective of an average person. Editors are great at giving feedback from an editor's perspective (that's their job), but because their training is such an integral part of how they view books, they may struggle to give you feedback from an ordinary reader's perspective. Alpha and beta readers can help you gauge how regular people might react to your book, giving you ideas about what you might need to change.

Top Tip: You can find alpha and beta readers through internet searches or through social media. Facebook and Reddit often have groups or threads devoted specifically to connecting authors with these specialised readers.

Wrapping Up

By now, you might feel a bit overwhelmed with all there is to know about editing. That's okay! It's a long, involved, complex process. That's why there are people who've devoted their careers to mastering it.

Like the work of other experienced professionals, editorial services don't come cheap. But editing is the one part of your book you can't afford to cut corners on. Readers might overlook a lacklustre cover or an inelegantly written blurb. But they won't cut you any slack on typos, characters they can't relate to or cliché plots. Remember, your book is competing with flashier, more quickly consumed forms of entertainment such as YouTube videos, games and social media. If your book doesn't hold readers' interest, they won't finish it – and may leave you bad reviews to boot.

Think of it this way: your book is your baby. You've put your heart and soul into it. You've done everything you can to nurture and develop it into the amazing thing you know it can be. But just as parents can't teach their own children everything they need to know to live productive, fulfilling lives, you can't produce a successful book all by yourself. It takes a village to raise both a child and a book. So, take a deep breath and start looking for your editors. The cost will be high, but it's an investment in future success. Your book – your baby – is worth it.

About the Author
Candice Bellows

Candice Bellows has been writing ever since she discovered that her colouring book didn't have captions, and she's been editing ever since someone first spelled her name *Candace*. A word of advice: don't. With that background and a complete sentence for a name, what choice did she have but to make words her career? Candice edited two historical monographs while earning a BA in English with an editing minor from Brigham Young University (BYU) in Utah, USA, and she's subsequently worked on elearning courses, fantasy novels, memoirs, business and finance books and guides for parents and teachers of young children.

Past employers and clients include Deseret Book, McGraw Hill Education, Six Red Marbles, Eschler Editing and Gryphon House. Candice published her first book, *The Year-Round Pillow Cover*, in July 2020. When she's not designing crochet patterns for her Etsy shop or trying to keep her own characters in one piece, she works as the Story Engineer, helping independent authors get from wherever they are in the writing process to publishing their books.

Connect Online
- **Website**: www.storyengineer.org
- **LinkedIn**: www.linkedin.com/in/candice-bellows
- **Facebook**: www.facebook.com/The-Story-Engineer-100737271563161
- **Instagram**: @storyengineer7
- **Twitter**: @TheStoryEngine1

N.M. THORN

THE Burns FIRE

Cover Design

Judging Books by Their Covers

Don't judge a book by its cover, they say...but don't we do this everyday? Every time a reader opens Amazon and types in their search words, at least twenty titles are presented on the first page immediately and that is not including all of the sponsored book adverts below.

If the reader is not searching for a particular book, what would make them click on the title of your book as opposed to one of the others? What stops their eye and draws their interest long enough to click on the link and explore further?

Ask yourself, how many times did you grab a book off a shelf in a library or a bookstore just because it looked cool? In most cases, it is because of the book cover. Think about your cover as a salesman who is pitching your novel to everyone who is searching online or browsing the bookshelves in a store.

The Anatomy of a Great Book Cover Design

In a way, *your book cover is like a billboard*. As you're passing it on a highway, you have just a few seconds to review the content. That short time is enough for you to form an opinion on whether you're interested in whatever the billboard is selling or not.

The same blink test approach can be used on your book cover; it has to effectively sell your book even if it is only glanced at briefly. Remember, your cover doesn't need to communicate all of the finer details at once, it simply needs to hook a reader enough so they are compelled to read your blurb and reviews to find out more.

So, let's review the main elements of a book cover and what makes it hold a reader's interest long enough to sell your story.

Respect Your Genre

Most readers know exactly what genre they want to read. They have their preferences, their likes and dislikes. So, when you are designing your cover, think about it from a reader's point of view. Your cover design shouldn't make them guess what genre your book is. Even worse – your cover should never misrepresent your genre.

Usually, good cover designs in each genre have certain types of colours, imagery, layouts and typography, so when readers look at your cover, they know exactly what kind of story to expect. Misrepresenting the genre can mean that potential readers may overlook your book. It could cost you quite a few unhappy readers who don't get what they are expecting and leave negative reviews. Sticking to the genre expectations can make all the difference.

Top Tip: Before starting with your book cover design, do some research and see what kind of elements would make your cover genre appropriate. Take a trip to a local bookstore or library or hit the Amazon search button and explore book covers in your genre. Visit the Top One Hundred list in the browsing categories that represent the genre of your novel. You will undoubtedly notice the elements and styles they have in common and this will help you start to formulate an idea of what will work well for your book.

Consider Imagery and Layout Carefully

Whether your cover features your main character or is typography centred, your design must create a natural flow of attention that would set a reader's focus on the most important point of your cover.

Balance is important in everything. The cover design is no exception to this rule. As much as you may be tempted to incorporate all the wonderful details of your story into your book cover design, you should refrain from doing so. Your cover must have air, so it is important to leave enough 'white space' (free space) so that it doesn't look too cluttered with lots of contrasting elements fighting for attention.

Taking a more considered approach allows the reader to concentrate on the most important elements of your design that best represent the story. An overcrowded cover is bound to lose a reader's attention almost immediately and will inevitably end up looking amateurish.

> **Top Tip**: Remember to think about how your design will look in a smaller size, such as a thumbnail on Amazon or a similar bookseller website. These online sites will most likely be your primary sales platform, so it is crucial for your cover to be impactful when viewed in this way. Do all the important elements still stand out? Can your title be read easily?

Typography

Typography is a vital element of a book cover, yet unfortunately it tends to be the most overlooked element of a design. However, any good book cover designer will tell you that the typography can easily make or break your design. All your font choices must be clear and easy to read, as well as eye-catching, visually interesting and appealing.

Just like everything else, typography must also be genre appropriate. For example, a handwritten script font could work well for a romance novel, but wouldn't be appropriate for a gritty crime drama.

When choosing fonts for your cover, limit yourself to no more than two fonts. Selecting more than two typography styles will make your cover look disorganised and unprofessional.

Readability

Your reader must be able to read your title, subtitle and your name easily, without straining their vision or trying to figure out the words among low contrast colours or curvy lines.

Visual Interest

Your cover must generate the wow factor at first glance, and typography is a powerful tool that would allow you to achieve this goal. The right combination of colour, texture and wise font choices can create a major impact with the book's title and other information on your cover.

Visual Appeal

While this sounds similar to visual interest, it is not the same. What may grab your initial attention is not necessarily what pleases your eye. If visual interest attracts the eyes, visual appeal will keep the reader looking at your cover for long enough to generate sufficient interest to read more about it.

Make It Stand Out

Remember, there is no second chance to make a good first impression. Choosing colours that stand out and grab a reader's attention is important. However, just like in everything else, balance is key. Vibrancy and contrast play a big part in drawing a person's attention and creating a certain mood and an emotional response.

We talked about the visual appeal above. While it is important for your colours to pop; they shouldn't hurt your reader's eyes. Pick colours that complement each other and work well together, making your design eye-catching and unique.

If you have a hard time choosing the colour scheme, or are not sure which colours would complement each other, you can consult a colour wheel tool. There are a lot of them on the market, but the Adobe Colour Wheel[22] is a popular choice.

> **Top Tip**: Open Netflix and take a look at their movie poster designs. You'll see right away what colours work well together, drawing your attention at a glance. Netflix is also well-known for using original typography that effectively reflects the theme of the movie or TV series.

Designing Book Covers in a Series

Book covers in a series must look like a family. By looking at the covers, the reader should have no problem identifying that they all belong to the same series. Even if the cover is character-centred and the main character is different in each book, keeping certain elements of the design similar, such as using the same typography, will help to create a recognisable series brand.

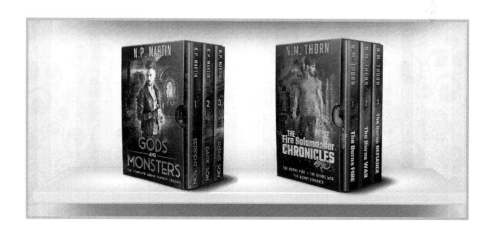

---

[22] 'Color Wheel,' *Adobe Color*, accessed 31 August 2020, https://color.adobe.com /create/color-wheel

DIY vs. Professional Covers

Design It Yourself (DIY)

If you decide to design your cover on your own, there are a variety of tools available on the market that would allow you to accomplish this goal, ranging from free options such as Canva and **www.diybookcovers.com** to more expensive, industry-leading programmes such as Adobe Photoshop and Adobe Illustrator. Another alternative is the free Cover Creator tool,[23] which you can access through the Amazon Kindle Direct Publishing (KDP) platform.

Canva is probably the most well-known, easily accessible tool. It is a free, web-based application for authors who do not have professional design skills under their belt. Canva is easy to use and it offers a variety of templates and stock photography.

The main advantage of taking a DIY approach is that it is undoubtedly cheaper. However, it can take significantly longer, as it necessitates learning the software and taking the time to use it properly, as well as researching all the technical details, such as the different file formats. All of this can be quite daunting for beginners.

Unless you have a high level of expertise in graphic design, or you can call on the help of an experienced friend or family member, you run the risk of the cover looking amateurish. This means that you could potentially lose out on sales as people tend to think that a poor cover reflects the book quality. Another downfall of using DIY tools is that the templates are non-exclusive, which means someone else could have a cover that looks very similar to yours.

Professional Book Covers

Most people are not in a rush to explore new, unknown authors. While that may sound harsh, can you imagine giving your time and money to an up-and-coming author who didn't invest in creating a beautiful cover for

---

[23] 'Cover Creator,' *Kindle Direct Publishing*, accessed 31 August 2020, https://kdp.amazon.com/en_US/help/topic/G201113520

their work? Most people see a professional cover design as a credible sign of a high quality writer, even if the two aren't necessarily correlated.

Creating an eye-catching book cover is not easy, and it requires certain skills and experience. Professional designers are not only adept with the Adobe Creative suite and other design software, but they also understand licensing law, the market and the requirements of different publishing platforms. They know how to put the colour scheme, imagery and typography together to create maximum impact and attract potential readers. Besides that, they understand genre requirements and stay on top of ever-changing book cover trends. All of that insight and expertise allows them to create an effective, polished cover design that works in your genre this season.

Hiring a Professional Cover Designer

So, you decided to hire a professional cover designer. But where do you start? You can find a number of suitable designers by searching on Google, visiting design marketplaces on Facebook or checking Instagram accounts. Asking for referrals from other indie authors or writing groups (online or in person) is another great way of finding reputable designers at reasonable prices. Ideally you are looking for someone with the vision and expertise to create an effective book cover, but who is also responsive and approachable when it comes to working with them.

However, there is more to the cover design than just pretty images and vibrant colours. Just because you have reviewed a designer's portfolio and liked a few designs in their gallery, it doesn't necessarily mean the designer will be right for you. Hiring a book cover designer is a serious step, so take your time to find a person whose work you love and who you feel comfortable working with.

Here are a few points you may want to discuss before choosing a designer…

Experience Designing the Book Covers in Your Genre

Most experienced designers have a website where you can find their portfolio of custom cover designs as well as their gallery of premade covers. Review them carefully and make sure that you like the design style. Besides that, make sure that the designer is experienced with the genre you are writing in.

If the designer doesn't show a lot of experience in your particular genre, but you like their design style, make sure they are willing to do the research and work on creating a genre-appropriate cover that is in line with the latest trends.

Design Process

Before you start working with a designer, make sure you fully understand their design process. Different designers may have a slightly different approach, so discuss it beforehand to know what to expect. Make sure that the research process, the communication style and the timeline fit your expectations.

Most designers offer a creative brief (survey) that will help them understand your vision of the cover. Some designers prefer to discuss this in more detail over the phone. Before you hire someone, take time to understand their research process and ensure that you are comfortable with their approach.

Availability

Many designers have their schedule booked for months ahead. Therefore, it is crucial to make sure that they are available to design your cover and complete it in a time that will allow you to meet your publishing deadline.

It is wise to start searching for a designer well ahead of your release date. Don't leave it until the last minute, otherwise you will only have a limited number of designers to choose from and inevitably it tends to be the better, more experienced designers who get booked up first.

Besides considering your designer's availability, keep in mind that it takes more than one day to create a cover, and, in most cases, more than one revision is done before the cover is ready and can be approved by the author.

Pricing

Make sure to review the designer's prices. Most people will have this information available on their website, but if they don't, do not feel uncomfortable asking. The cost of book cover design services varies between different designers and you need to make sure that their pricing fits your budget.

The costs could vary from $50 per cover to $1,000 or more. There are quite a few contributing factors that can affect the price, such as the experience and reputation of the designer and how much work is involved to create a certain type of cover. For example, timely photo manipulation or a complex illustration design can legitimately drive up costs, as can the use of premium stock photography.

Custom or Premade? That Is the Question

To answer this question, first you need to understand what the difference is between custom and premade book covers.

Custom Book Covers

Custom covers are created by the order of the author with their specific creative vision of the design in mind. Custom covers are usually elaborate, detailed and highly relevant to the book's content.

Premade Book Covers

Premade covers, by comparison, are created in advance by a designer, often with a genre in mind but without being attached to a particular story. Usually, premade book covers are presented in a designer's online gallery for an author to buy. When a premade cover is purchased, a designer will change the text (title, subtitle, tag line and author name) on the premade cover, however the details of the design will remain the same.

While premade book covers are not custom tailored to your story, they are still done by a professional designer, look genre appropriate and are visually compelling. If your budget is limited, a premade book cover could be a great starting point, since they are a lot cheaper than a fully customised design. They also tend to be a quicker alternative because the lead time can be a lot shorter as the majority of the work has already been done.

One Final Thing

Once you select your designer and discuss your vision of what you are looking for, try not to micromanage them. Trust their expertise and allow them to use it to create an effective cover that will make your book stand out and make a notable impact.

Any good professional designer wants your book to succeed. For them, it is a matter of professional pride as well as extra exposure. When they work on your cover, they want it to be not only beautiful but also a perfect selling tool. Keep in mind that in general, designers are creative individuals, so while explaining your vision of the cover, give them some space for their creativity to blossom. You won't be disappointed.

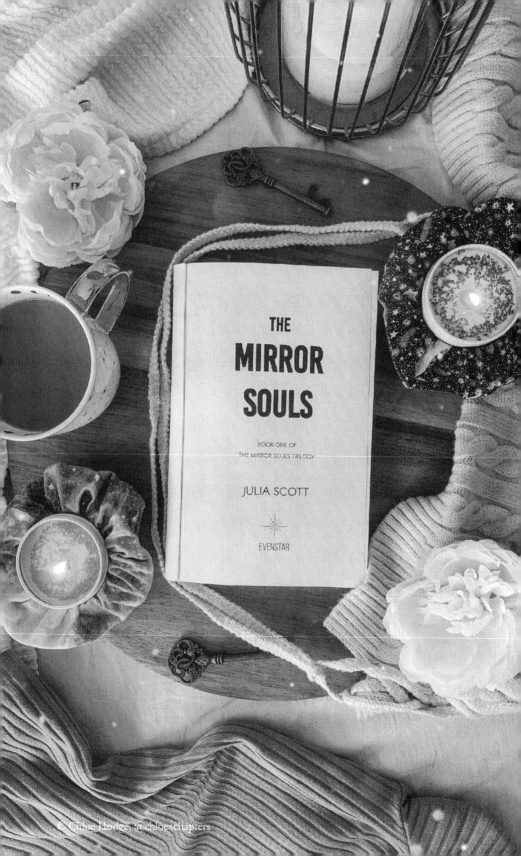

THE
**MIRROR
SOULS**

BOOK ONE OF
THE MIRROR SOULS TRILOGY

JULIA SCOTT

EVENSTAR

Formatting
by Julia Scott

The Importance of Interior Formatting

Now that your beautiful book has gone through draft after draft, been edited to near perfection and proofread to weed out those sneaky typos, it's ready to go out into the world. Right? Well...not quite.

Your next challenge, should you choose to accept it (although, you kind of have to), is to prepare your manuscript so it is ready for printing and distribution. Unfortunately, it's not quite as simple as throwing a Word document at Amazon and hoping for the best. Not if you want a beautiful and professional looking book that is!

As with most steps from first word to published book, formatting can either be undertaken by a paid professional or you can choose to take it on as a Do It Yourself (DIY) project. There are pros and cons to both.

Pros of Hiring a Formatter:
- They already have the knowledge required to turn your words into a beautiful book and know how to resolve issues that crop up along the way.
- They understand how the print-on-demand and e-book services work, and their specific requirements.
- They usually have a good eye for design and know what works and what doesn't in book interior design.
- It saves you time, as it can be a lengthy process learning how to do formatting well.

Cons of Hiring a Formatter:
- It is an extra expense that can potentially be avoided.
- If you need to make changes to your manuscript, such as small edits or adding your new titles to the front and back matter, you'll often need to pay your formatter to make those changes.

- You are reliant on their schedule and pre-booking a time slot to get your work done.

Pros of DIY:

- It saves money, keeping your publishing costs down and your profits up.
- If you need to make changes to your book at any time without extra costs incurred, you can.
- Your work can be formatted when it's ready, rather than having to fit into someone else's schedule.

Cons of DIY:

- The steep learning curve, especially if technology isn't really your 'thing'.
- It can often take more time (and involves more stress) than you might expect.
- Initial software costs depending on which program you choose.

For the sake of this chapter, let's assume first that you're taking the DIY route. We will cover both physical book and e-book formatting, design choices to consider, what to avoid, share a little bit of how-to knowledge and identify valuable resources. Even if you do choose to work with a professional formatter instead of attempting it yourself, some of these points will also help you when deciding who to work with and how to communicate your design preferences with them.

Physical Book Formatting

Why Is Interior Formatting Important?

We all know the popular phrase, 'Don't judge a book by its cover.' But how many times do we end up picking a book because we think, 'Oh my goodness, that cover is so gorgeous!' Now imagine picking up that stunning book, excited and already enamoured, only to open it up and see a hot mess. The fonts are weird, there are odd spaces where they shouldn't be, the margins are 'off' and there are no page numbers.

Okay, so that's an extreme example. But it would put you off, right? The absolute main goal for the interior of any book, even aside from being visually attractive, is to not be distracting. Formatting that makes your book easy to read and keeps your reader engaged in the story, rather than being distracted by oddities in the layout, is a job well done. The pretty chapter headers and fancy fonts are simply the icing on the cake. The readability of your words is key.

> **Top Tip**: Before you start designing the interior of your own book, take a trip to your local library (or your bookshelf) and check out the books in your genre. Flip through the pages, get a feel for what design elements and types of fonts are common in that genre. Make sure to look at recently published books for the most up-to-date design trends.

Software for Formatting

Which software you decide upon as your weapon of choice for formatting will depend on several factors, including budget and what type of computer you have access to. There are pros and cons to the various types, but ultimately you will be able to produce a fantastic looking book with any of these, as long as you put the work in where required.

Your main software choices are:

- **Word Processing Software** (e.g. Microsoft Word and Open Office)
- **Design Software** (e.g. Adobe InDesign)
- **Book Specific Software** (e.g. Vellum)

The most common choice is Microsoft Word or an equivalent, as most people with a computer will own it already and know how to use it. Word is generally frowned upon by those seeking 'industry-standard perfection,' but it can still produce beautiful books. It has its quirks and frustrations, but once you know how to deal with them, it's quite a simple process.

Those who are aiming for 'industry-standard' will typically go for design software like Adobe InDesign. There is a much steeper learning curve with this software, which is lessened if you already have experience with other Adobe products such as Photoshop. InDesign is set up for book formatting and design, so the tools you need are easily accessible and the result is high quality. There are plenty of online courses and step-by-step YouTube videos available that will help you create a great looking book.

Another option you may have heard of is Vellum. This is a plug-and-play type software specifically designed to create print books and e-books in minutes. It is a costly option, but worth doing if you're planning on publishing many books and lack the technical knowledge and/or patience for Word or InDesign. Vellum has limitations in what you can do design wise, but if you're only after simple design elements, then it is more than adequate. The biggest downside is that it is only available for Apple Mac computers.

Book Sizing

You're in the driver's seat and in control of the way your book looks, and size is going to be the first decision you make. How large do you want your book to be?

5 x 8   5.25 x 8   5.5 x 8.5   6 x 9

Here are the most common book sizes (in inches) that are used in both traditional publishing and self-publishing:

- 6" x 9"
- 5.5" x 8.5"
- 5.25" x 8"
- 5" x 8"

Of course, there are many other sizes that you could choose, but these are the most popular industry-standard sizes and are the ones that the print-on-demand services such as Amazon Kindle Direct Publishing (KDP) and Ingram Spark will provide.

My recommendation for choosing a book size is to take a ruler over to your bookshelves and see what sizes your favourite books are. Which size book do you like to hold in your hand? Most people have a preference. Interestingly, there are differences regarding what is popular depending on where you live. In the USA 6" x 9" is generally the most popular book size, whereas in the UK most traditionally published books are smaller, usually closer to 5" x 8".[24]

One thing to take into consideration is the length of your book. If you've written a tome of 250,000 words, you'll need the largest book size (within reason), otherwise the book will have far too many pages. It will either be impossible to print by the restraints of the print-on-demand company you're using, or it will look ridiculous. On the opposite end of the spectrum, a novella of 30,000 words is going to make for a very skinny book in the larger sizes so you may want to consider sizing down.

The second consideration is whether your book is going to be part of a series or not. So yes, you may have written a novella that would look silly in a 6" x 9" size, but you might want it to match your full size 100,000-word novel that you have planned. So perhaps it's wise going for the size in between the largest and smallest in order to keep your series consistent.

---

[24] 'The Most Popular Standard Book Sizes in the US and UK,' *InDesignSkills*, 27 July 2018, www.indesignskills.com/tutorials/standard-book-sizes

Templates

An easy way to get started with formatting your book is to find a template for Word or InDesign, in the size you require for your book. This will have all the margins pre-set so that you can just put your text in place and go! Basic templates can be found for free online, usually by companies who want to sell you other products or services.

As a professional interior formatter, I know how impotant this first step can be to avoid undue hassle and pain later on. So, I have created a range of paid-for templates at the following website **www.thebookformattingformula.com**, all of which come with short tutorial videos that explain how to use them.

Be Prepared

Regardless of which software you use to format your book, you'll need to tidy up the raw file holding all your text first. This is likely to be in word processing software. Even if you're going to be moving your text from here into something like Vellum or InDesign, it's wise to get the file as clean as possible to avoid errors when you do import it. This is important for importing into software that creates e-books too, so don't skip this step!

Start by removing text elements that shouldn't be there. The standard for any kind of book is to only use a single space in between sentences rather than a double space. An easy way to change this, or to weed out any accidental double spaces, is to use the 'Replace' feature on a word processor. It's as simple as replacing all double spaces with single spaces.

Another common formatting no-no to avoid is using tabs at the start of each paragraph. Remove these by using the 'Replace' feature, replacing all tabs with nothing. Then change the paragraph settings for the whole document to put indents for the first line of each paragraph instead of using a tab. The only exception to this rule is paragraphs that denote a scene change or are at the beginning of a chapter are not indented, which you can manually change afterwards.

If you are using Microsoft Word for your formatting and not using a template, it can be helpful to create a new document to set up for your final formatting, rather than making changes to the document that already contains your text. This way you can make sure all the settings are correct and save it as your own template for future books.

Creating Beautiful Text: Fonts

The world of fonts is vast. You may not even realise quite how vast if you are the type of person who usually sticks to Times New Roman! I'm pretty sure I could write an entire chapter about fonts, but let's assume you just want the basics to make sure you don't step wrong.

Serif vs. Sans-serif

Make sure to use a serif font when writing large paragraphs of text, what we call the 'body text,' and not a sans-serif font. How do you know the difference? A serif font has the little strokes on certain letters, whereas sans-serif does not.

Serif

Sans Serif

A serif font is easier on the eye to read and is industry-standard across the board when it comes to publishing. Sans-serif fonts have their place for titling and chapter headers etc., especially for non-fiction or modern books, but not for reading whole blocks of text. The only books that traditionally use san-serif fonts for body text are young children's books because it is easier to read, but crucially these stories only have one or two lines per page so it works alright in this context.

If you've ever seen an entire printed book written in a sans-serif font like this one, you'll realise how odd it looks and how distracting it is to read, which is what we are trying to avoid!

Great serif fonts for body text:

- Baskerville Old Face
- Garamond
- Georgia
- Goudy Old Style
- Palatino Linotype

Avoid Overused Fonts

You might think that sticking with the fonts you know can only be a good thing, but when choosing a font for titles or chapter headers, think outside the box. There are many fonts that have been overdone and are quite the turnoff, especially if you're after a unique and interesting design for your book. As I mentioned before, the world of fonts is vast, so you should have no problem finding a great font that fits your genre and suits your story.

On the avoid list:

- Arial
- Calibri
- Comic Sans
- **Impact**
- Papyrus
- Times New Roman
- Viner Hand

The following image showcases *Seek Me* by Nyla K. Two decorative fonts were used for this design. One for the chapter title and drop cap, and the other for the subtitle and header. Two contrasting fonts is enough to bring interest, but not too many to overwhelm the senses.

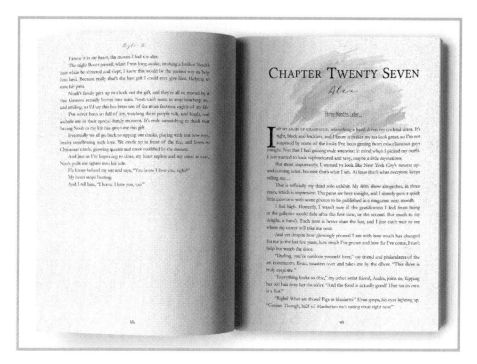

Font Matching

A great way to bring cohesion to your overall book design is to use the same fonts found on the outside of your book, inside your book. If you've had a cover designed by someone else, ask if they'll let you know which fonts they used. If for any reason they won't tell you, then you could always try to find one that looks similar. It may take some internet trawling, but it'll be worth it.

Where to Find Fonts?

There are many places to find free and/or paid-for fonts online. My favourites are:

- www.dafont.com
- www.fontsquirrel.com
- www.creativemarket.com

Licensing of Fonts

Be mindful of font licensing when downloading a font to use from the internet. Some fonts are listed as free for personal use only. Some are demos. Others don't have the full range of characters required (such as numbers or exclamation marks).

There are plenty of fonts that are 100% free, but the extra awesome ones can cost money. Most fonts that you download from the sites listed above will contain a readme.txt in the zip file when you go to extract the font. Read this to make sure you are licensed to use that font for commercial purposes.

Creating Beautiful Text: Sizing, Spacing and Layout

Font Sizing and Spacing

Once you've chosen a font, there are other choices to make that will determine how your overall text will look. First, you'll need to decide on a font size. The size of the font affects the readability so you want to avoid going too small or too big. The genre of your book can influence this too as books for younger readers tend to have bigger font sizes, but not by too much, so don't go over the top. In general, fonts tend to be between 10 and 12 pts for body text. Bear in mind that a 10pt size in one font can look much smaller compared to 10pt in another font. Half points work too, so try 10.5pt if 10 is too small and 11 is too large.

The next choice is regarding line spacing. The spaces between each line of text will also impact readability. A general rule of thumb is that single line spacing is too tight and 1.5 line spacing is too loose. Use pts as line spacing (in Word, this is the 'Exactly' option on the Line Spacing drop-down list) and try out pt numbers until you find something that works well for your page size. If you're unsure, look at a book you own that is the same size as yours. Count how many lines are on each page and try to emulate that with the spacing of your own text.

In fiction, paragraphs tend not to have gaps in between them and will match the same line spacing as any other line in the text. If you have larger gaps, it can be distracting, as it leads the reader to create a mental break in the way they read it, in the same way a comma causes a reader to pause in a sentence. Leave bigger paragraph gaps for scene breaks.

Both font size and line spacing will contribute to how many pages your finished book will be. If you're trying to keep it below a certain number of pages due to printing costs, consider a smaller font or slightly tighter line spacing. But as with everything, don't overdo it and make your book difficult to read.

Paragraph Settings and Page Layout

Choosing margin sizes is another parameter that will contribute to the number of pages your book will end up with. The wider the margins, the less text you can fit on a page. Every page has three outside margins (top, bottom and side) and one inside margin (also called the gutter). Margins ensure your text isn't cut off during manufacturing. The inside margin will change depending on the number of pages in your book, because thicker books need a wider gutter, so keep that in mind too. Self-publishing platforms, such as Amazon KDP, have more information on their Help pages to make sure you know the minimum margin sizes required.[25]

Paragraphs need to be set to indent on the first line. This is especially important for fiction where there are no breaks between paragraphs. Again, try different size indents out, but the size I tend to go for is 0.8cm.

Make sure to justify your text, rather than left align it. This will make the text line up on both sides of the page, which is industry-standard and looks far neater. The more advanced design software, such as InDesign, include an option to justify the majority of the body text while left aligning the last line in every paragraph, which helps to avoid loose spacing.

Choose whether to start your pages on the right-hand page or not. This is a personal choice and sometimes the design of the chapter header page lends itself well to all chapter pages starting on the right. This will inevitably leave some blank pages, which pushes up the page count, so bear that in mind.

When it comes to non-fiction, the rules tend to be a little more flexible. Sometimes non-fiction books will have spaces between each paragraph and no first line indent. Whatever you choose to do, make sure to be consistent across the book.

---

[25] 'KDP Help Centre Home,' *Kindle Direct Publishing*, accessed 31 August 2020, https://kdp.amazon.com/en_US/help

> **Top Tip**: Once you've chosen your fonts, sizes and spacing, print off one page of full text at 'actual size' to see how it looks. Cut the paper to the size you have chosen for your book, for example 5" x 8", and compare it to a book you already have of the same size. Does it look right? If not, tweak it until you're happy with it.

Don't Overdo It

One final, but no less important, point to remember about fonts is 'less is more.' Do not bombard your reader with ten different fonts! Font choices need to be purposeful and enhancing to the overall design and not be distracting. Choose one or two fonts maximum for your headings, such as chapter number and subtitle, and one font for your body text. In some cases, you could use another font in the body text to show phone text messages or internet chat room messages for example. But keep it simple. The reader is there for your wonderful story, not for a font showcase or showdown.

Other Design Elements

Images

Aside from fonts, there are other decisions to be made and elements to pull together to ensure you have a professional and beautiful book ready to buy.

Whether or not you put images in your book is down to personal choice. Again, it can be dictated by genre, but there are no hard-and-fast rules. Chapter headers, scene breaks and page numbers are the common choice for adding a little extra illustration to bring interest to your book. Maps and character art can also be fantastic features, especially for fantasy novels.

A few technical tips:

- Any images you use should be at a minimum resolution of 300ppi (Pixels Per Inch). This is the optimal resolution for digital printing presses to avoid images becoming blurred or pixelated.
- If you are using images that have a transparent background, save them as a PNG instead of a JPEG, otherwise the image will print with a weird translucent box around it.

- Make sure your images look good in black and white, unless you're printing a colour interior (which can be costly!)
- If you want your images to go right to the edge of the page, you'll need to select the 'bleed' setting when you upload your file. This means the page size of your file will need to be slightly bigger than the finished page size, with the margin adjusted to compensate, so that the pages can be trimmed when printed.

My advice regarding images in books is the same as with fonts; less is more. Avoid overdesigning and distracting from the important part of your book: the words. Again, as with fonts, it is helpful to bring elements from your cover design into the interior for cohesion. This can be as simple as using similar shapes that are used on the cover or general imagery. It doesn't have to match exactly.

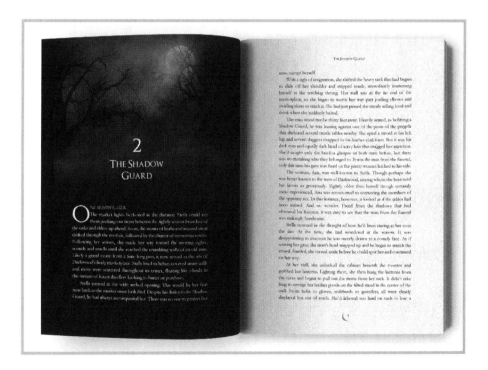

The image above showcases *The Dark Wood* by Sydney Mann. This design features a full page, dark image underneath white font for a striking chapter page that is related to the story.

Headers and Footers / Page Numbers

Some authors choose not to include a header in their book, but many will use this space for the book title on one page and the author name on the other. An alternative use of the header is to indicate the chapter name or the character point-of-view, instead of the book title and author name.

Page numbers are most commonly found at the bottom of the page in the footer, but you could choose to include them in the header instead. It's up to you! Again, check out books in your genre to get a feel for what others have done.

E-book Formatting

In many ways, even if you're lacking in the technical skills department, e-book formatting is easier than physical book formatting. Generally, readers who buy e-books tend to expect less in terms of design compared to those who purchase a paperback or hard cover copy of your book. The wise move is to keep it simple.

E-book File Formats and Software

There are several file formats that you'll come across when learning about creating e-books:

- **.ePub** – used for most e-book readers, such as Kobo
- **.kpf/.mobi/.azw/.azw3** – used for Kindle
- **.pdf** – Adobe PDF

ePubs are the generic file type used for the majority of e-readers except for Amazon's Kindle. There are two free software choices that you can download: Sigil and Calibre. These will convert Word documents to ePubs very easily. If you're using InDesign, there is a built-in feature to convert your books to ePubs, but be warned – there are many little tweaks required to make sure it converts properly, especially if you're using chapter headers and images.

Kindle has its own file types; mobi and azw are the main ones. Amazon has created a program called Kindle Create[26] which makes creating

---

[26] 'KDP Help Centre Home,' *Kindle Direct Publishing*, accessed 31 August 2020, https://kdp.amazon.com/en_US/help

beautiful Kindle e-books a breeze. However, there is a downside to be aware of. This software creates a kpf file type, which is uploaded straight into KDP. If you want to give your Kindle e-book away to someone for free as an advanced reader copy (ARC) prior to your publication date, you won't be able to send them this file type, it will be useless. It also cannot be converted to a mobi file type due to DRM (digital rights management) that Amazon has built into the kfp file type. Instead, you'll have to create a mobi file type using software such as Calibre, in the same way as ePubs.

PDFs can be read on most types of e-reader, but they aren't reflowable (so the text won't adjust depending on the reading device). Most ePubs and Kindle formats are reflowable, which means that when the font size is changed, the text shifts and fills the screen regardless of the size. PDFs cannot do this, so you're not able to change the font size at all.

And finally, if you own a Mac and you've chosen Vellum to format your physical book, you're in luck. Vellum will also produce beautiful e-books with the click of a button. By default, Vellum will generate files for individual e-book platforms (such as Kindle, Apple and Kobo). If you choose to upload to an aggregator (such as Draft2Digital or Smashwords), you can create a generic ePub too.

Where to Get Help?

Amazon KDP has a very comprehensive help section with a wide range of tutorial videos that explain what is required of finished files for uploading to their platform. Ingram Spark can be a little more complex, but they are easy to contact to ask for advice. Other platforms should have similar measures in place to help their users.

And the master of self-help, YouTube, is full of videos showing how to format books with Word, InDesign and other software.

If you get stuck, try not to throw your computer out of the window. Take a deep breath and seek out help. It will all work out in the end.

Professional Formatting

You may be thinking that there is no way you'll be able to figure out how to get your manuscript beautiful and print-ready all by yourself. Perhaps you feel daunted by the time required or the technical skills you would have to learn to go down the DIY route. And that's okay! If you feel like this, finding a professional formatter may be a wise approach for this part of your book's journey.

When you are searching for a professional formatter to work with, bear in mind that each have their own style and set of specific services. Some purely focus on getting manuscripts print-ready, keeping the design elements to a minimum. Others can bring more graphic design into your book to really make it stand out, for example by enhancing the chapter titles in a creative way. Others can draw illustrations from scratch to fit your story perfectly.

But where to find them? Many formatters list their services on websites such as Fiverr.com, others can be found from a simple internet search. It is also worth asking other authors on social media or in writer networks for recommendations. Whoever you decide to work with, make sure to check out their testimonials and look at examples of their work to make sure you like their style and feel that they can produce a final formatting look that fits your story and genre.

The image above showcases *Vengeance Blooms* by Chloe Hodge. Working with an illustrator can help bring your book's interior design to life and really reflect the story. Chloe Hodge worked with artist Emily Johns to create a chapter header and decorative page numbers.

Each formatter will work differently, but the basic process will involve discussing your design preferences with them, choosing which size book you want to go with, then sending them your manuscript (usually in a .docx format) for them to work their magic. The formatting process is likely to go much smoother if you get your document as clean and tidy as possible beforehand – see the 'Be Prepared' section earlier in this chapter. They will likely send you some design ideas based on your consultation with them to make sure you are happy with the design elements and fonts before they go ahead and format the whole manuscript.

When choosing a formatter, make sure to check out their prices and find out what is included in that price. Will they provide an e-book format as well as paperback? How much would it cost for further edits to be made in case you stumble across any pesky typos? Ensure there are no hidden extras that will cost you more later.

If you want an option that is somewhere in between creating your book masterpiece from scratch and hiring a professional to do it for you, there are also web-based services online that are almost as plug-and-play as something like Vellum. One such free service is provided by Reedsy.com, which will help you produce both print and e-book formats. The design of your final product will be fairly basic with this service, and not overly customised, but it's an affordable and time saving option.

Conclusion

Formatting your manuscript brings you one step closer to holding your book in your hands, which is one of the best feelings as a writer. Regardless of whether you choose to format your book yourself or work with a professional, remember: keep your genre in mind, less is more when it comes to design work and fonts, and don't hesitate to reach out and ask for help and advice wherever you can get it.

About the Author
Julia Scott

Julia Scott is a British indie author whose goal is to take you out of 'regular life' and teleport you to new worlds and alternate futures through her writing. *The Mirror Souls* is her debut novel, and like many sci-fi and fantasy books, it started off as a dream. The second book in the series, *The Anahata Divide*, was released in 2020.

In her 'other' life, Julia lives in Essex, England with her husband and two children. She spends her time mum-ing, writing, prettifying books (via her formatting business Evenstar Books), graphic designing (a range of author products are available on Redbubble), singing, and planting or digging stuff up in the garden without really knowing what she's doing.

Connect Online
- **Websites**:
  - o www.juliascottwrites.com
  - o www.evenstarbooks.com
  - o www.redbubble.com/people/Evenstarbooks
- **Facebook**:
  - o www.facebook.com/juliascottauthor
  - o www.facebook.com/evenstarbooks
- **Instagram**:
  - o @juliascottwrites
  - o @evenstarbooks.juliascott

EVENSTAR
BOOKS

"I loved this book. It's a really great read; a proper whodunnit! As a debut novel, this is a cracker!"
JOY ELLIS, No.1 bestselling author of the *D.I. Nikki Galena* series

MURDER AT MACBETH

Whose deadly secret has taken centre stage?

International Flash 500 Novel Award Longlist

Samantha Goodwin

Book Launch Tips
by Samantha Goodwin

Making Your Best First Impression

So, you've officially finished your novel – congratulations! But before you get overexcited and rush into your release, it is worth taking the time to properly plan your promotional activities to help make your book launch a success. This is particularly crucial for indie authors who usually coordinate a lot of the launch themselves and don't have the luxury of a big advertising budget, which can make it considerably harder to get noticed. After all, over 2.2 million books are published every year,[27] so it is vital to make sure that yours stands out right out of the gate.

A Note About Marketing

Marketing really does need to be taken seriously – how else are readers going to find out about your book? It goes without saying that you should absolutely utilise all of your own author social media channels to support your launch, such as Facebook, Instagram, Twitter and if you are an authortuber; YouTube. I would definitely recommend being active online with meaningful content on launch day. I've been utterly confused by some authors when they haven't even mentioned their new book release until weeks later.

Plus, if you have an author website, blog, newsletter, podcast or if you have patrons on Patreon, now is the time to use these platforms to help spread the word. You could also consider online advertising such as Pay-Per-Click (PPC) adverts on social media or sponsored adverts on Amazon. As you may have gathered, marketing is a huge topic and I'd recommend familiarising yourself with the following Book Marketing chapter that

---

[27] Piotr Kowalczyk, 'Which Countries Publish The Most Books?' *Ebook Friendly*, 6 April 2017, www.ebookfriendly.com/countries-publish-most-books-infographic

contains lots of helpful advice that I won't be repeating here regarding maintaining the momentum of your marketing activities. What I will be focusing on is all the additional launch tips I have learned over the years that should help you plan an effective book release.

Do Your Research

The great thing about launching a new book is that plenty of authors have been in your shoes before and can be very forthcoming about what worked well for them and, perhaps even more importantly, what didn't.

As well as researching handy tips online, you can also check out numerous Facebook Groups that have thousands of fellow writers who you can connect with and a treasure trove of information. I've found some more particular useful ones are the Indie Author Group, Writers Helping Writers and World Indie Warriors.

Set a Realistic Budget

Before you get carried away planning loads of activities, it is wise to carefully consider what your goals are and to set a realistic budget for what you hope to achieve. The budget requirements for an indie author who aspires to become a full-time writer will be very different than someone who has written a book that is predominantly intended for their friends and family.

Although, don't panic if you don't have a huge budget – I've included lots of free approaches in this chapter that can help get your book noticed without costing the earth. Consider this a 'Pick and Mix' style approach; don't be overwhelmed by all the options available, you can simply choose just to use the approaches that are most appealing to you.

Author Endorsements

Endorsements from other authors can go a long way to help with the initial reception of your book, especially if it is your debut novel. There is a reason all the books you see in bookshops have glowing endorsements printed on their covers; they provide legitimacy and social proof, helping potential readers to trust the new author.

Therefore, it is really important to ensure that you start the process of requesting endorsements early enough to incorporate into your book cover design, promotional materials and online listings. In order to do this, be mindful that you will need to be prepared to send out Advance Reader Copies (ARCs) of your book, usually in a Kindle Mobi, ePub or preview paperback format.

Which Authors to Ask?

Ideally, endorsements are most meaningful when they are from authors who write in a similar genre as you do. Their reputation means your target readers would be more likely to trust their opinion and crucially they are more likely to enjoy reading your book. In terms of who to ask, it would be really helpful if you had already built up genuine connections with other authors beforehand, for example through networking at writing conferences or engaging in online communities.

At the very least, make sure you reference why you admire the author and are choosing to get in touch with them. I always include an Advanced Information Sheet with my initial queries too (more on that later). From my experience this approach definitely seems to work well as I found a number of authors were happy to read an advanced copy of my debut novel and I received positive feedback about my enquiry method:

> "I did want to congratulate you on the most perfect pitch approach I've ever seen – including the numerous press releases that accompany the tens of proofs I'm sent every week. The content and tone are both textbook – I'm so impressed!"
> **CLARE MACKINTOSH,**
> **The Sunday Times Bestselling author of** *I Let You Go*

What Type of Endorsements Work Best?

Author endorsements are most compelling when they are *credible*, *specific* and provide *a call to action*. Now, of course you are at the mercy of what people choose to say, but it is helpful to be mindful of these points when selecting which quotes to include on your book cover. Personally, I would recommend a minimum of three endorsements; one for the front cover and two for the back. Normally these would be short, edited quotes, with the full longer endorsements in the review section at the front of your book. Let's look more closely at each of these three themes, one by one.

Credible

As my debut novel, *Murder at Macbeth*, was a contemporary murder mystery, it made sense for me to approach other crime writers. Coincidentally, be bold about who you ask – you might be surprised who agrees to read an early review copy. I'm still thrilled that I got my book into the hands of Joy Ellis, an internationally renowned crime author who has sold over two million books!

"I loved this book. It's a really great read; a proper whodunnit!
As a debut novel, this is a cracker!"
JOY ELLIS,
No.1 bestselling author of the *D.I. Nikki Galena* series

"Excellent writing, with a strong, compelling hook."
LORRAINE MACE,
author of the *D.I. Sterling* crime series

Specific

Endorsements are much more impactful if they indicate what the reader can expect or can incorporate a clever play on words so that the unique review quote simply would not make sense on any other book cover.

"*Murder at Macbeth* entertains in true *Poirot* style.
It's a classic whodunnit with a real period feel to it.
It read like a really good episode of a prime-time crime series."
CAROL DEELEY,
author of the *Britannica* series

"Goodwin's debut whodunnit novel truly takes centre stage!
Just when you think you have the mystery solved,
she drops the curtain on you. Such a fun, suspenseful read!"
DANIE JAYE,
author of *The Lions* trilogy

Call to Action

Call to Action is a common term in marketing and, simply put, it means what action you would like someone to take after reading something. In this respect, good endorsements help to create a sense of urgency that compels people to buy your book. This could be by appealing to the fact that it is a 'must-read,' or the endorsement could imply when the book could be read, such as 'the perfect holiday read.'

> "*Murder at Macbeth* is an absolute page turner, filled with fascinating characters and plenty of twists and turns. This is a quick, fun, entertaining read for a summery poolside day or a cosy winter afternoon."
> **JULIA J. SIMPSON,**
> author of *Ashes Swept*

Giving Something Back

It is always good practice to try and give something back to all the authors that help to provide early endorsements as a thank you. This could be anything from sending out signed copies to doing feature posts or author interviews on social media to show your appreciation and help raise awareness of the authors' own works.

Entering the Blogosphere

Book bloggers are simply fantastic! Avid readers who will not only jump at the chance to read your book, but also spend time writing or filming comprehensive reviews to inform other people about it; what's not to love? You can also request bloggers get involved in promoting your cover reveal, as well as hosting giveaways, author interviews and guest posts. All great options for raising awareness of your new release and it can help get the ball rolling on Amazon and Goodreads reviews too.

Before you get in touch, always check the blogger's review policy on their site to ensure that they accept self-published (or indie) books, they are interested in your genre and they are currently accepting new review requests. The review policy should also state what Advanced Reader Copy (ARC) book format they require if they are interested in your review request. Bear in mind that you will need to budget carefully for print and postage costs if you commit to sending out paperback copies, as it can get expensive fast. Although in my experience, I found many bloggers readily accepted free Kindle Mobi or ePub files.

How to Find Book Bloggers and Vloggers

So, how to discover these elusive book bloggers, I hear you ask? Well, you have a few options that you could explore…

Indie View: www.indieview.com

This is a really useful resource that collates a searchable database of bloggers who review indie books and lists their genre preferences.

The Book Blogger List: www.bookbloggerlist.com

There are a number of websites that collate useful lists of book bloggers that you can peruse to discover people who may be interested in your book. One of the best is *The Book Blogger List* that collates a large number of blogs categorised by genre. You will however have to consult the review policy on each blog to see if they accept indie books.

Blog Rolls

Check the blog rolls on book blogs so you can discover related sites. This is a list of recommended links, usually on either the right or left side of the main homepage.

Genre-specific Blogs

Research blogs and websites that are specific to the genre you write in who might be interested in featuring your book.

NetGalley: www.netgalley.com

If you have budget available, you may find it worthwhile paying for a listing on *NetGalley* that provides free early review copies to book reviewers and bloggers.

Facebook Book Blogger Groups

These are some fantastic Facebook groups that connect authors directly with book bloggers. *Book Connectors* is a good one to start with.

Social Media

Social media is another great tool for connecting with book bloggers. You can use specific hashtags to identify people who might be interested and put out your own posts calling for interested bloggers to get in touch.

Remember to include relevant hashtags so your post is more visible and your reach extends beyond your followers.

Here are a couple of Instagram hashtag themes you might want to try to get you started:

Book Blogger Hashtags:
- #Bookstagram
- #BookBlog
- #BookBlogger
- #BookBloggers
- #BookBloggerLife
- #BookBloggersLife
- #BookBloggersOfInstagram
- #BookBloggersOfIg
- #BookBloggersOfInsta
- #BookBloggersWanted
- #BloggingAboutBooks

Book Reviewer Hashtags:
- #BookReviewersOfInstagram
- #BookReviewers
- #BookReviewersofInsta
- #BookReviewersOfIG
- #BookReviewersWanted
- #BookReviewersNeeded

Taking the Direct Approach

Another great way of finding bookstagrammers who would be interested in your book is to search on social media for book or author hashtags of similar titles in your genre. For example, my debut crime mystery novel is often likened to Agatha Christie's *Poirot* and the Paula Hawkins books, *The Girl on The Train* and *Into the Water*, so I can search for hashtags featuring these to discover people who like reading these types of books. I've made contact with numerous bookstagrammers using this method who have been delighted to read and review my book and post about it on social media.

Interacting with readers of the genre you write in also helps to circumvent the tricky Instagram algorithms too as it can make your profile become more visible to like-minded readers who may want to connect with you. One trap a lot of indie authors fall into is posting so much about writing that Instagram automatically categorises them as only being interested in writing accounts. While it is useful to have a circle of author friends online, ultimately it is the target audience of your book you should be seeking to connect with on social media. Some authors even take this matter into their own hands and create two accounts; one to focus on their books and one to connect with other authors.

To Pay or Not to Pay

Paying for reviews is a somewhat divisive topic amongst indie authors. Some people swear by paying for initial reviews, but personally I'm firmly in the camp of seeking honest free reviews. Not least because paid reviews can violate Amazon's terms of service and you really don't want to be blacklisted on Amazon!

If you do pay for reviews, then I believe you can include short snippets from these in the editorial section on your Amazon book description and of course you can use these quotes in your promotional materials and social media posts. Do make sure you do your due diligence because it's very easy to be ripped off or be caught out by scams.

Other indie authors that I know have been impressed with the following paid review sites. Although please do research thoroughly and make your own judgement call, especially as I can't personally vouch for these:

- **The Book Bag**: www.thebookbag.co.uk
- **The Book Review Directory**: www.bookreviewdirectory.com
- **BookViral**: www.bookviralreviews.com
- **Indie Reader**: www.indiereader.com
- **Kirkus Reviews**: www.kirkusreviews.com
- **Literary Titan**: www.literarytitan.com
- **Online Book Club**: www.onlinebookclub.org
- **The Prairies Book Review**: www.theprairiesbookreview.com
- **Publishers Weekly**: www.publishersweekly.com
- **Readers Favorite**: www.readersfavorite.com
  Free review option available too (but review is not guaranteed).
- **Self-Publishing Review**: www.selfpublishingreview.com

Competitions and Awards

Success in book competitions or achieving literary awards can be another useful way of gaining credibility as a new indie author. Such plaudits clearly signal to prospective readers that your book is a high quality read. You may be interested to learn that there are loads of well respected, international novel competitions that you can enter, some of which are exclusively for debut authors and others which celebrate achievements in indie publishing. Amazon even run their own free annual competition for all books that are published through their Amazon KDP programme.

But, before you run off and enter all the writing competitions you can find, do consider the one main drawback of this approach; cost. Most competitions or awards charge entrants a fee to enter and the cumulative cost of entering multiple ones can quickly spiral out of control. I'd recommend taking a considered approach and work out what your budget is beforehand so you don't get carried away.

Personally, I tend to cherry-pick which competitions I enter but have found that the recognition gained from the ones I did choose came in handy for my book launch. My debut novel was longlisted for the *International Flash 500 Novel Award* before it was officially published, which meant I could promote that achievement on my book cover and on social media. Later recognition came from achieving a *Gold Literary Titan Award*, *Chill With a Book Readers' Award* and an *Indie Author Central (IAC) Five-Star Reader Rating*, all of which contributed towards further enhancing my credibility as a new author.

Recommended Author Awards and Contests

Below I've collated some of the more preeminent awards and contests that exist for indie authors. All of these have been rated and reviewed as recommended by the watchdog desk of the *Alliance of Independent Authors (ALLi)*.

The *Alliance of Independent Authors* monitors the self-publishing industry by vetting services that align with their code of standards and identifying rogue services which can overcharge, over-promise, under-deliver or, in any way, exploit authors. For more information, please visit **www.selfpublishingadvice.org**.

Please note this is not an exhaustive list of awards and do make sure you check the relevant websites for up-to-date information:

- **B.R.A.G. Medallion**: www.bragmedallion.com
- **Book of the Year Awards (Independent Author Network)**: www.independentauthornetwork.com
- **BookLife Awards (Publishers Weekly)**: www.booklife.com
- **Independent Book Publishers Association (IBPA) Ben Franklin Awards**: www.ibpabenjaminfranklinaward.com
- **Indie Author Project Contest**: www.indieauthorproject.com
- **Kindle Book Awards**: www.thekindlebookreview.net
- **Rubery Book Award**: www.ruberybookaward.com
- **Self Publishing Review (SPR) Awards**: www.selfpublishingreview.com

Social Media Exposure

At any given time, there are bound to be loads of online initiatives on social media that you can get involved with – you simply need to keep your eyes peeled for the latest available opportunities. When I was in the process of launching my debut novel, I participated in the *Women Writing Fiction Exchange* where authors from all over the world showcased each other's work through their own platforms. I've also been involved in an international *Indie Authors Against Hunger* campaign that involved collaborating with a large group of authors promoting each other's books and donating all of our proceeds to food bank charities for a month.

New initiatives are popping up all the time, so do keep a lookout and remember you can explore some of the indie book hashtags on social media to discover current initiatives.

I've outlined some of the recurring themes that I'm aware of on the next page if you wanted to check them out.

Indie April: #IndieApril
An annual month long celebration of indie books on social media.

Indie Author Day: www.indieauthorday.com
Every year on 7th November, libraries and organisations around the world welcome local indie authors in for a day of education, networking, mingling, writing, panels and much more.

Indie Pride Day: #IndiePrideDay
Every year on 1st July, indie authors from around the world take to social media to share photos of themselves holding up their books.

Indie Feature Friday: #IndieFeatureFriday
A weekly showcase to review and promote indie books every Friday.

Self Promote Sunday: #SelfPromoteSunday
Initiated by author Julie Embleton (@julie_embleton), Sunday marks a weekly invitation to indie authors to share their work on social media.

Indiecember: #Indiecember
An annual reading challenge in December hosted by author Megan Tennant (@_megan_tennant) which showcases a wide range of indie books.

World Indie Warriors: www.worldindiewarriors.org
A supportive community of indie authors who collaborate to run various initiatives, including a regular ebrochure featuring a wide range of indie books and international members' video meetings held on Zoom.

Indie Book Cover Competition: @samanthagoodwinauthor
A free annual competition to celebrate amazing indie book covers with lots of exciting prizes up for grabs every year. It opens for entries in March on my own Instagram account.

Indie Writing Wisdom: #IndieWritingWisdom
Hosted by myself on Instagram, this is a regular showcase of inspiring, original writing tips shared by indie authors to motivate fellow writers.

Advance Information Sheets

An Advanced Information (AI) Sheet is a tool used by traditional publishers to help promote books pre-publication by providing a straightforward, concise summary of the key details. As an indie author, I found this to be extremely helpful when approaching book bloggers, the media, independent bookstores and other authors.

There is no industry standard dictating how an Advanced Information sheet should looks, but they are generally in a single A4 page format and include similar content, which is summarised below. Do make sure that the book title and author name are very clearly displayed at the top of the page – these need to be unmissable.

Main Content to Include:
- Book Title
- Book Cover Image
- Author Name
- Endorsements
- About the Book
- About the Author
- Key Selling Points

Book Details:
- Genre
- Release Date
- Price
- Distributors
- ISBN

Contact Details:
- Email Address
- Telephone Number
- Author Website
- Author Social Media Channels

Check out the following Advanced Information Sheet for my debut novel, *Murder at Macbeth*, to get a sense of what this can look like once it is all pulled together.

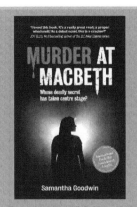

Release date: 17th May 2019
Genre: Crime mystery
eBook: £1.99 ($2.99) or
Free on Kindle Unlimited
Paperback: £7.49 ($8.99)
ISBN: 9781798960707
Available on Amazon

"I loved this book. As a debut novel, this is a cracker!"
JOY ELLIS, No.1 bestselling author of the *D.I. Galena* series

"A classic whodunnit that entertains in true Poirot style. It read like a really good episode of a prime-time crime series."
CAROL DEELEY, author of the *Britannica* series

"Excellent writing, with a strong, compelling hook."
LORRAINE MACE, author of the *D.I. Sterling* crime series

For more information, free review copies or interview requests, please contact the author Samantha Goodwin:

Email Address

Telephone Number

https://samanthagoodwinnet.
wordpress.com

MURDER AT MACBETH

Samantha Goodwin

About the Book

Whose deadly secret has taken centre stage?

When a talented, young actress unwittingly stabs herself live onstage after a prop knife is tampered with, suspicion immediately falls on her eclectic band of castmates.

But who had the motive to kill the show's leading lady?

As the insightful, yet disillusioned, Detective Inspector Finley Robson and his shrewd partner, Detective Sergeant Nadia Zahra, interrogate the seven key suspects, secrets unfold to unveil a web of scandal, blackmail, and deceit.

Bitter rivalries, secret trysts and troubled pasts are just the beginning of the story…

INTERNATIONAL FLASH 500 NOVEL AWARD LONGLIST

About the Author

Samantha Goodwin has written professionally for her business career as a Chartered Marketing Manager for over a decade before turning her hand to fiction. As an avid crime fiction fan, she regularly participates in the renowned *Theakston Old Peculier Crime Writing Festival* in Harrogate and relishes attending literature festivals across the country as well as engaging in numerous online writing communities.

Keen to support new and upcoming authors, Samantha recently launched the *#IndieWritingWisdom* initiative on Instagram to collate and share inspiring, original writing quotes from a wide range of different writers to encourage others. When not writing, Samantha enjoys reading, movies, musicals, countryside walks and almost all chocolate (but controversially not Oreos). She lives in Leeds, England with her husband, Chris, and young son, Jack. *Murder at Macbeth* is her first novel.

The Tricky Thing About Book Promotion

As a Chartered Marketer, with over a decade of experience in the industry, I'd like to think I know a thing or two about promotion. Interestingly, one of the main developments over the past years is that as people have become increasingly savvy and knowledgeable, no one wants to be 'sold to' anymore. For few products is this more true than books. Readers quite rightly want to choose what they add to their To-Be-Read pile and not feel pressured into making that decision. Which poses a bit of a dilemma for authors who want to spread the word about their books.

So, what to do? Well, the good news is that as a writer you're in a great position to capitalise on two of the major buzzwords in modern marketing: *relationship building* and *content marketing*.

Essentially, in an author context, this means developing meaningful relationships with potential readers and sharing creative content that does not explicitly promote your book, but is intended to stimulate interest in it. Believe me, this approach can also be a lot of fun as a writer. Listed below are a few creative ideas you might like to try out.

Cover Reveal

An official cover reveal on social media can help engage potential readers and create excitement around your upcoming release. This is a great opportunity to be creative and encourage people to share your cover reveal on their own channels too.

Release Date and Pre-Orders

Following your cover reveal is a great time to announce the official release date of your book and open up pre-orders. Do make sure you build in buffer time though to account for any unexpected delays.

Creating a Buzz

There are tons of inventive ways you can build anticipation around your release, from special price promotions to offering the option to pre-order signed copies through your author website. Another tactic is to provide limited edition book merchandise (or book swag, as it is affectionately known), such as bookmarks, signed book plates or character prints.

You could also do a launch countdown on social media, reveal excerpts in the run up to release day and even host an online launch party too.

Content Is King

Remember what I said about content marketing being the way forward these days? As a writer you are perfectly suited to crafting creative, engaging content that helps to entice potential readers. Consider posting short excerpts or character interviews on social media as something that is quirky and interesting. Likewise, I've seen fantastic examples of authors sharing pictorial moodboards, music playlists and even vocabulary definitions for new lanugages they have created.

Remember you can also create interesting videos in addition to written content, such as author interviews or live Q&A sessions.

Book Trailer

Cinematic book trailers are a growing trend, and they can be very effective as they often provide the first glimpse readers get of your story. A mesmerising vignette of your book that leaves a lasting impression on the viewer can complement your other book launch activities perfectly.

Video marketing statistics tell us that 85% of internet users in the United States watch online video content on any device.[28] Therefore, an

---

[28] J. Clement, 'Online video usage in the United States - Statistics & Facts,' *Statista*, 30 September 2019, https://www.statista.com/topics/1137/online-video/

interesting book trailer can provide an ideal way to reach new readers, expand your fanbase and increase sales through improved engagement.

As an indie author, you'll probably find that studio-quality videos cost too much money and time to produce. Even large traditional publishers rarely see these as a necessity, instead opting for simple trailers that are just as effective in generating tangible interest in the book.

However, there is a wide range of affordable indie author book trailer services that you can explore, just be sure to check out their showreel on their website to ensure you like their style before committing. Or alternatively, there is also various video maker software, such as Adobe Spark and Apple iMovie or specific apps like Biteable, Blender or Canva that you can use yourself to create a captivating trailer for a fraction of the cost.

Be sure to invest time in learning the necessary skills if you do go down the DIY approach; a poorly executed video trailer would probably harm your reputation as a new author even more than if you didn't have one in the first place.

The Writer Behind the Books

Readers love talking to authors. Help start the conversation and host *Ask the Author* sessions on social media, go live on Facebook or Instagram to directly answer questions, share short videos about yourself and your writing process or create *Get to Know the Author* posts to provide behind-the-scenes insights. Social media is exactly that: social. People are on these channels to engage with others, so focus on building a community rather than just follower numbers.

Go on Tour

Nationwide book tours of travelling to multiple cities are fast becoming a relic of the past, replaced now with virtual book tours that see authors visit a new blog each day – ideal for indie authors with less budget at their disposal. Online content can vary from book reviews, author interviews, excerpts, a guest post, a book giveaway or a combination of all of these. A blog tour can be a powerful tool to reach new audiences and drum up support for your upcoming release.

> **Top Tip**: You have the option of paying for a Blog Tour company who will coordinate everything on your behalf, or you can contact book bloggers directly yourself. For my own launch I did the latter and found bloggers to be incredibly receptive – over 50 featured my book! So the free approach can definitely work, albeit start planning well in advance and be prepared to take a long time liaising.

Book Signings

Explore the opportunity to set up a book signing in your local bookstore (such as *Barnes and Noble*) or library. These can be excellent events to help raise awareness, meet prospective readers, drive more book sales and provide local publicity. Many bookstores plan their in-store calendar several months in advance so make sure you get in touch early and ensure that there will be physical copies available to sign on the day.

Involve Your Fans

It is a great idea to involve your fans so they can cheer you on and help spread the word about your new release. Some authors choose to formalise this and form an exclusive Digital Street Team who help to create a buzz online. I've been part of such a team for another author before and we all received a simple media kit that proved helpful to coordinate our book blitz activity for sharing cover reveals, book blurbs and giveaways.

After all, many people find out about new books from their peers, so it can be a helpful approach. Ideally you should reward your street team in some way too, for example by providing exclusive content, early reader copies, social media shoutouts or special discounts.

Create an Original Campaign

It's always good to try something different and one of my all-time favourite promotion ideas was to create an Instagram World Book Tour that encouraged readers from all over the world to share photos of my book using the hashtag #MurderAtMacbethWorldBookTour.

The campaign quickly grew beyond my wildest dreams and, as a UK author, it has been incredibly exciting for me to see my book travel to 51 countries and 34 US states. This has included a myriad of far-flung, exotic destinations I've not even visited yet myself, such as Australia, Hawaii, India, Indonesia, Lebanon, Mexico and the Philippines to name but a few.

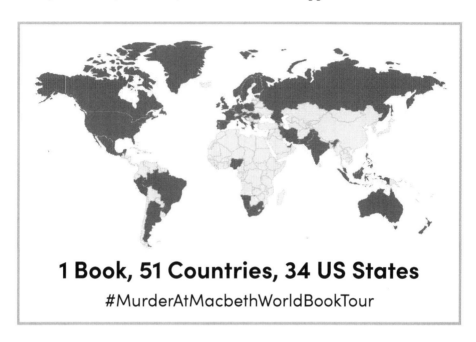

1 Book, 51 Countries, 34 US States

#MurderAtMacbethWorldBookTour

Giveaways

Personally, I'm a huge fan of book launch giveaways to celebrate new releases. Who doesn't love the chance to win a signed paperback or a shiny new e-book? You can host your own giveaway on social media or collaborate with book bloggers or bookstagrammers who can significantly extend the reach of who has visibility of your competition.

There are some important points to consider when hosting a giveaway:

- **Use relevant hashtags**. This is crucial so people can discover it, #bookgiveaway and #bookgiveaways are a must. But don't stop there – research further to discover more related hashtags.
- **Keep it simple**. People have short attention spans online so they are likely to scroll past anything too complicated. Ideally, I would recommend simply asking people to follow your channel, like the post and comment to enter. Then you can offer extra entries to people who tag others and share in their social media stories.

- **Make the prize obvious**. Be clear from the onset what the giveaway prize is and, as few people will be familiar with your book, it's handy to include your book blurb and some review quotes.
- **State if it is international**. Make it obvious if the giveaway is open internationally or is restricted to your own country.
- **Remember the legal bit**. It is good practice to use a short legal disclaimer too, something along the lines of, 'This giveaway is in no way sponsored by or affiliated with Instagram.'

The Art of Self Promotion

The fact remains: no one can buy your book if they don't know about it. Consequently, the single most important goal of your book launch activities is to raise awareness of your new release and introduce yourself as an author. In addition to connecting with book bloggers and harnessing the power of social media, here a few other things you could consider to get your name out there.

Author Interviews

You would be surprised how many bloggers, authors and book websites are open to publishing author interviews, which provides perfect free promotion. I ended up doing over 30 interviews to coincide with my own book release and found it to be a lot of fun. You can explore opportunities for written interviews to be published on various sites, in addition to considering podcasts, vlogs or even live interviews on social media platforms, such as Instagram or Facebook.

Guest Blogs

Another great tactic for helping to promote yourself as an author is to seek out opportunities to write guest posts on existing blogs. This is an ideal way of showcasing your writing talent and helps to raise awareness of yourself and your books to an already established audience. This can be a good first foray into blogging and can be a useful approach for those authors who feel they can't commit to maintaining their own blog.

Newsletter Swaps and Group Promotions

One useful method of engaging with people and collaborating with fellow authors is to consider doing newsletter swaps or group promotions where you organise promoting other people's books so they can return the favour.

There are a number of Facebook Groups and websites you can subscribe to in order to connect with other indie authors who write in your genre. Sites to check out include BookFunnel, StoryOrigin and Prolific Works. In addition, these sites also allow you to set up direct email integration and create customised landing pages, allowing readers to easily sign up for your mailing list and download free e-books.

Of course, you could always team up with other indie authors you already know to do cross promotions to reach a wider audience together. There can be strength in numbers, especially when you're a new author, so collaborating with more established authors can be a great approach.

Guest Speaker Events

Plenty of authors also have a great personal story to tell and so it would be ideal for them to speak at local schools, literature festivals, conferences or events. This is a great way of reaching a new audience and could be combined with a book signing too.

Book Clubs

If you can arrange it, getting involved with book clubs can be a great way to expose your book to more readers and generate increased sales. You can be creative with how you appeal to book clubs, such as by including discussion questions at the end of your book or as a free download guide from your website, or by offering exclusive discounts for book club members.

The novelty factor of attending a book club as a special guest to facilitate an Ask the Author discussion can also be a great draw. I know plenty of indie authors who have attended local book clubs in person and really enjoyed the experience. But with the growing use of video technology, there are also an increasing number of opportunities to be a virtual guest, which means you can interact with book clubs from all over the world from the comfort of your own home.

Book Subscription Boxes

Another fantastic promotional opportunity that can help launch your novel is to get involved in a book subscription box. These provide a range of exciting new fiction books to readers on a regular basis, often accompanied by popular swag items like bookmarks, candles, pens and notebooks. The contents of the boxes are a mystery until they are received and unboxed by excited customers. Alongside genre-specific boxes, there are a growing number of subscription box opportunities that focus entirely on indie authors, such as Indie Book Connect and Indie Book Box.

The book subscription craze adds an exciting and fun dimension to the online literary community. They can be useful for authors because not only could you expand your target audience by getting your novel into the hands of numerous book-loving subscribers, but you could also benefit from enhanced engagement and promotion online as readers and bookstagrammers are encouraged to share about their boxes on social media.

However, my only word of caution is to carefully work out all of the associated costs before you agree to be involved. I've been approached by two subscription box companies who wanted to include my debut novel, which was really flattering, but unfortunately the cost of shipping hundreds of signed copies from the UK to the USA made it unfeasibly expensive so sadly I had to decline the offers on those occasions.

Have I Got News For You

While approaching the media might sound like a daunting prospect, it is actually surprisingly easy. As long as you present yourself professionally you don't really have anything to lose. Your gamble might just pay off and win you much sought-after press coverage. I even know indie authors who have managed to secure interviews on national TV programmes, including *The One Show*, and prime-time radio shows because they had a compelling story to share. The key is to carefully consider what is newsworthy about your book release and then adapt your approach accordingly for different audiences so your query is more likely to get noticed.

A few important points to remember when writing a press release for the media:

- **Write a catchy but informative headline.** Journalists get hundreds of emails daily so you will need to stand out.

- **Always include a professional, high resolution photograph.** Ideally this should be of the author with the new book. Most newspapers refuse to run a story without an accompanying photograph.
- **Include contact information.** The journalists need to be able to easily get in touch with you if they require any further information.
- **Begin with the key information.** The journalist should be able to quickly grasp the story just by reading the first paragraph.
- **Write in the right style.** A press release should be written as a news story. Focus on facts and keep sentences short and simple.
- **Include a quote.** Journalists like quotes so it can be helpful to incorporate at least one into the press release, even if it is from yourself.
- **Always proofread.** Make sure you run a spellcheck before sending.

Top Tip: For my own book launch, I secured a lot of regional newspaper and online coverage from various outlets by tweaking the angle of my press release to best suit the target audience. For example, the *York Press* newspaper ran the story with the headline that I was a former Easingwold Secondary School student, whereas *South Leeds Life* newspaper stated I was a local resident and the *Made In Shoreditch* website referenced that area of London was the setting for my novel.

Try Before You Buy

Inevitably, if you are a new author, you do pose a risk to potential readers. Even with glowing endorsements and book blogger recommendations, it still takes a leap of faith to pick up a debut novel. Luckily there are lots of things you can do to help mitigate this risk so people feel more confident in investing in your book.

Free Opening Chapters Download

One simple way of getting readers drawn into your story is to offer a free download of your opening chapters from your website or when they sign up to your newsletter. This can be provided as a formatted PDF and is very simple to set up. However, do be mindful not to contradict any conditions from your book distributor (which can often limit the amount of chapters that you can offer for free).

Opening Chapter Published on Book Blogs

Another similar tactic is to collaborate with book bloggers so they publish your opening chapter and book blurb on their sites, usually to accompany an author interview or review. Bloggers usually have a much larger audience than an author alone, so it can be really helpful to work together so you can reach more people.

Look Inside Feature on Amazon

On Amazon it is very straightforward to set up a *Look Inside* Feature that enables readers to see a preview of your book so they can read the first few chapters online and assess if they would like to buy the full book afterwards.

Prequels

Another fantastic strategy is to provide a free prequel that helps hook readers into your world and give them a taste of what is to come. This is particularly helpful when introducing a new series and has been used to great effect by numerous indie authors.

Hitting the Number One Spot

Just a cautionary warning that it is worth keeping a close eye on the different Amazon category Top 100 lists for both e-books and paperbacks following your official launch. The rankings are updated hourly and so it can be very easy to miss if you do make it into the Top Ten List or hit the coveted Number One Spot.

It may only be fleeting, but it is certainly exciting while it lasts. On my launch day, my debut novel, *Murder at Macbeth*, made it to the Number One spot in multiple categories on Amazon. For a brief time, my paperback even ranked higher than Anthony Horowitz's Sunday Times Bestseller, *Magpie Murders*, in the British Crime Books Bestseller List, which is definitely my favourite claim to fame.

While I've Got Your Attention

So, you've got your book into readers' hands – *success*! But don't miss this opportunity to cross-promote your other books, including ones that are upcoming in the series. It is great practice to include book blurbs and reviews at the back of your book. After all, if people enjoyed the read then they may well be keen to seek out your other works. Equally, don't be shy to include a polite request to readers that if they enjoyed the book then you would really appreciate it if they left a review on Amazon or Goodreads.

Have Fun and Celebrate

You wrote a book! You should be so proud of that fact. According to the *New York Times*, 81% of people (or Americans at least) would like to write a book,[29] but only a fraction ever actually do. In fact, it's a well-quoted statistic that 97% of writers never finish their novels.[30]

If you have got as far as planning your book launch, then you have already achieved something monumental. Now is the time to have fun and celebrate. Enjoy your moment of publishing a new book.

---

[29] Joseph Epstein, 'Think You Have a Book in You? Think Again,' *The New York Times*, 28 September 2002, www.nytimes.com/2002/09/28/opinion/think-you-have-a-book-in-you-think-again.html

[30] K.T. Anglehart, '97% of Writers Don't Finish Their Novels: 5 Steps to Be Part of the 3% and Write a Book in 10 Months,' PolishedPages, 12 October 2018 (updated 15 February 2019), www.polished-pages.com/post/write-a-book-in-10-months

About the Author
Samantha Goodwin

Samantha Goodwin has written professionally for her business career as a Chartered Marketing Manager for over a decade before turning her hand to fiction. As an avid crime fiction fan, she regularly participates in the renowned Theakston Old Peculier Crime Writing Festival in Harrogate and completed their prestigious Crime Writing Creative Workshop. She relishes attending literature festivals across the country as well as engaging in online writing communities.

Keen to support upcoming authors, Samantha originated the #IndieWritingWisdom initiative on Instagram to collate and share inspiring, original writing quotes, does a weekly #IndieBookSpotlight and has launched a new annual Indie Book Cover Competition.

When she is not writing, Samantha enjoys reading, walking, movies, musicals and almost all chocolate (but controversially not Oreos). She lives in Leeds, England with her husband, Chris, and son, Jack.

Murder at Macbeth is her first novel and it centres around a talented, young actress who unwittingly stabs herself live onstage after a prop knife is tampered with. Suspicion immediately falls on her eclectic band of castmates, but who had the motive to kill the show's leading lady?

Connect Online
- **Website:** www.samanthagoodwinnet.wordpress.com
- **Instagram:** @samanthagoodwinauthor

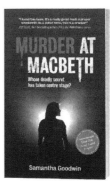

Book Marketing
by Michelle Raab

Getting Started with Marketing

You're an indie author, which means that you are responsible for everything from writing your fabulous novels or short stories, to getting your work ready for publishing, to marketing your work. The previous chapter summarised some great book launch techniques, but what do you need to do marketing wise when you're not releasing your book? Where do you even begin? Not knowing where to start can make marketing feel very overwhelming.

As a Book Marketing Professional, what I tell my indie author clients is to *start where you are*. It's never too early to start marketing, and it's never too late. You can start when you're flirting with the idea of becoming an indie author. You can start when you're going to release your book. You can shift gears and start anew after releasing ten books. Just start where you are. So, phew.

You're in exactly the right place you need to be to market yourself and your work. But, what exactly do you do? There's so much advice out there, it's hard to know what to choose, and there's so much jargon it's difficult to understand what everyone is talking about.

This is not a comprehensive look at indie author marketing because, quite honestly, I could write volumes on it. This is an overview of marketing concepts that will help you get started in creating your own marketing plan, in addition to introducing a range of different tactics you can use to help raise awareness of your book and generate sales.

Marketing Plan Formula

Your marketing plan is essentially a step-by-step guide of how you are going to engage in marketing activities to promote your book. Underpinning your marketing plan is your **strategy**, which is why you have chosen certain goals and then you use different marketing **tactics** to accomplish your goals. I know that you can do this. You have done something much more complicated, which is writing a book. Just follow the Marketing Plan formula and you'll be well on your way.

Let's start with the formula:

> **Strategy** (why you are choosing the goal)
> **+ Goals** (what you want to achieve)
> **+ Tactics** (how to achieve those goals)
> **= Results**

You can also look at it like this:

1. **Pick a strategy.**
2. **Pick a goal based on the strategy.**
3. **Pick a tactic to achieve the goal.**
4. **Measure your results.**

Whether it's easier for you to think about this as a formula or a list of steps, you can use them to create the outline for your marketing campaign.

Before you can dive into making your marketing plan, it is helpful to have a bit more information about how these different elements work. Let's start with some basic ideas in marketing.

Marketing Strategy and Goals

Your main objective for creating your marketing plan is for people to read or purchase your book. For some indie authors, they want readers to buy their books in the hopes of breaking even on the cost of publishing. Others want their writing to be a side-gig and an additional source of income. Still others want to be full-time writers. What all of these desires have in common is making sales. Therefore, your marketing plan needs to include goals intended to move potential readers closer towards buying your book.

Marketing Goals: A Reader's Journey to Purchasing a Book

It is helpful to consider the journey to purchasing a book from a reader's perspective, since ultimately, they are your target audience. This shouldn't be too hard because every writer started out as a reader.

A reader likes to read. They probably have a few favourite genres and story tropes. I know that I do. I'm sure that you do too.

If you're in the mood to buy a new book, what do you do? Either visit a bookstore or go online and browse a bookseller's website. You type in some keywords and you're immediately presented with a list of possibilities. You might be drawn to a few that have interesting titles or intriguing book covers. You may look at the description, read the summary and peruse through some reviews. If you're still interested, you may read a chapter. If you like the sound of it, you buy it.

Another way that you may search for new books is to look up recent favourite reads on bookseller websites to explore what related titles other people have purchased. You may even have a favourite author, so you research their other books or explore similar authors.

What I'm describing here is what marketers call the **consumer buying cycle**. It's also known as a *sales funnel* or the *purchase intent stages* and a bunch of other names.

Originally theorised as five stages,[31] I've reduced it to three for simplicity:

- **Purchasing Stage 1**. A reader has a desire to read a new book, so they search for books to read and then evaluate alternatives.
- **Purchasing Stage 2**. The reader decides which book to read.
- **Purchasing Stage 3**. The reader buys the book.

Knowing about this sequence of events is helpful in terms of focusing your marketing goals. A clear marketing plan begins with a clear goal.

Purchasing Stage 1

As an indie author, there's not much you can do about influencing people's desire to read a new book, but there's a lot you can do to let them know that your book will satisfy their desire. The first step is letting them know that you exist. This is called **brand awareness** or name **recognition**.

---

[31] John Dewey, *How We Think*, Courier Corporation, 1997. First published in 1910, then in 1933.

Broadly speaking, brand awareness happens in a variety of ways. One way is that a potential reader knows you by name so they can specifically search for one of your books and purchase it.

Alternatively, you can also gain brand awareness by being connected with other books that are similar to yours, which is why your book appears on the 'people also bought' lists on bookseller websites. This connection is *learned* by the bookseller's algorithm, which is looking for buying patterns.

In these two scenarios, I have described two very different marketing goals. One goal is that *readers* have brand awareness. The other is that an *algorithm* has brand awareness. The bigger goal is for your book to be known, but the target is different: potential readers versus an algorithm.

In the first scenario, in order for potential readers to develop brand awareness you need to be promoting your book to your target audience. There is a whole range of different tactics you could implement in order to achieve this goal, which are covered in more depth later in this chapter.

The second scenario is getting the algorithm to recommend you. Algorithms are automatic systems that look for and learn about patterns in data and are constantly being updated. For algorithms to recommend you, it is important for fans in your genre to write reviews so it can learn to associate your book with them. It is equally important to get these reviews on bookseller sites, such as Amazon, rather than just on review sites like Goodreads.

In your marketing plan, you can set two goals to increase brand awareness:

- **Strategy 1**: You want to target potential readers who are in the first purchasing stage and don't know that you exist.
- **Goal 1**: Brand awareness of you and your book.
- **Tactics**: Combination of marketing tactics to promote to your target audience. An example is *content marketing* where you tell your target audience about yourself and your book.

- **Strategy 2**: Get bookseller algorithms to know your genre so they will recommend your book to readers browsing similar books.
- **Goal 2**: Connect your book to booksellers' databases so the algorithm will recommend you.
- **Tactics**: Research relevant keywords for your book description and metadata on bookseller websites and encourage readers, especially of your genre, to leave reviews.

Purchasing Stage 2

The next stage in the buying process is when the **reader makes the decision to buy your book**. At this stage, they've decided they want to read a new book and are aware your book exists, but aren't yet convinced enough to purchase it. Here they will evaluate your book and other titles to see which book will best fill their desire to read.

When considering whether to buy a new book, readers tend to look at the title and the cover, consult the reviews, read the blurb and maybe even read the first chapter. This is called the *considering* or *evaluation* stage. You want a potential reader to say 'yes' to your book based on this information.

A potential reader may love the genre you wrote in, but not care for the tropes you used. Maybe they love romantic suspense, but don't like the 'enemy to lovers' trope. If that's the case, they will keep looking, unless there is something else about your story that overcomes that preference.

To make sure they choose your book and enjoy reading it, the story needs to be well crafted, have believable and engaging character arcs, flowing prose and continuity, and it needs to be edited well with no plot holes or typos. This is especially important when you're paid by the number of pages read in an e-book, such as on Kindle Unlimited, as people can stop reading at any point if the book falls short of their expectations.

Pay attention to how you start your book. Since part of the reader's evaluation will likely include reading your first chapter in the online preview, it becomes a selling tool. They want the action to start right away, so they are hooked and want to read on to know what happens next. These days there are multiple forms of entertainment and you want readers to choose your book, so make sure that your first chapter really grabs them.

- **Strategy**: Stand out from other similar books in your genre.
- **Goal**: Readers say yes to your book.
- **Tactics**: Enticing book cover, compelling blurb, well-written book, engaging first chapter, providing a sample chapter, pricing, branding promotion and positive reviews on bookseller websites.

Purchasing Stage 3

This is the final stage of the buying process **when the reader purchases your book**. Do bear in mind that if it is an e-book sale where you get royalties from pages read, making sure people keep reading is essential to your profits. If you plan on writing more than one book, make sure you're known for spinning a great tale.

Coincidentally, writing multiple books could be considered a marketing tactic in itself because loyal readers who have enjoyed your first release could be keen to come back for more. The money and time involved in attracting repeat readers is usually considerably less than attracting new readers.

- **Strategy**: Get readers to commit to purchasing the book.
- **Goal**: Readers buy your book and don't return it.
- **Tactics**: The first chapter is written to be a sales tool and draws in the reader immediately. The book is well-written with good and engaging pacing, interesting characters, no typos or grammatical mistakes, and is generally a page-turner.

Marketing Tactics

Marketing tactics are the **different approaches you can take in order to promote your book** and achieve your goals. Authors usually take an integrated approach and utilise a number of tactics simultaneously.

Branding

All the things that make up your brand is what makes you different. **Your brand is the keystone of your marketing strategy**. I've worked with many indie authors who are not quite sure what a brand is or how to establish one. I often get the impression that many people think it's simply an author logo, but your brand is much more than that.

Your brand is the story of *how your voice and your books are different from others like it*. A brand is a complex concept. It is a combination of a lot of things, like why you want to write, your unique point of view, your voice and how well-written your stories are.

Your brand is *your story*, as told by you, the media and readers. **Branding is *the way you tell* your story** through visuals like logos, your content marketing (such as blog posts and social media), advertisements and your books.[32]

So, how do you tell your story? There are many different tactics you could use, which we are going to explore next.

Promotion

Promotion is **what you do to gain brand awareness** of yourself as an author and your books in order to influence potential readers and make sales.

Content Marketing

Content, in a general sense, is anything that is posted online, ranging from You-Tube videos, excerpts on Instagram, blog posts or character quizzes on social media. Content marketing, then, is using online content to market your book.

The good news is this type of promotion is free, you are in complete control of the narrative and as an author this probably plays well to your creative strengths. The cost here is the time it takes to create high quality content and the consistent effort it takes to build and maintain a loyal following. Crucially, the emphasis should be on sharing great content that resonates with your target audience, *not* just talking about your book all the time.

There are a number of different channels you could utilise to communicate your story through effective content marketing, which are discussed in more detail next.

---

[32] For further information, consult 'Branding: Starting from Scratch,' *Michelle Raab Marketing*, 18 May 2020, http://bit.ly/brand_raab1

Social Media

Social media platforms have different strengths, depending on your marketing goals and the demographic of your target audience. This tactic is very flexible in that it can be used for establishing and maintaining your branding awareness and for targeting any of the purchasing stages. Current options include Facebook, Instagram, Twitter, YouTube, LinkedIn, Pinterest, TikTok and even Snapchat. Trends are always changing and so are the social media platforms so it is definitely worth doing your research before rushing into setting up your accounts.

Deciding which social media channels to focus on depends on where your potential readers hang out online, what you're comfortable doing and what you have time for. If your target audience is middle-aged women, then you'll probably want to spend more of your time on Facebook. If your target audience is GenZ, then you'll want to spend more time on TikTok.

You can easily conduct an online search to find out the social media preferences of your target audience. Since these trends change frequently and new social media platforms continue to emerge, I recommend you look this up when you're developing your marketing plan.

Consider your time restraints carefully as you will generally find it is better to invest in running a few social media accounts really well than to stretch yourself too thinly across multiple channels.

> **Top Tip:** Remember you can use hashtags in your posts that readers may follow on social media, such as #toberead, #bookworm and #bookdragon, which is a good way of reaching your audience and getting noticed. However, hashtags are always evolving so spend some time exploring what the most appropriate options are to use.

Blog

Creating an author blog can be another effective content marketing tactic and certainly lends itself to your writing abilities. However, posting frequently is key to driving engagement and contributing to good search engine optimisation (SEO) so people can find your blog. SEO is a big topic. Because search engines find and list found items according to the rules of an algorithm, every time search engine companies (like Google) tweak their algorithms this sends digital marketers into a tizzy. Keeping up to date on current trends of keywords and methods for your SEO is essential. It would be wise to write a lot of interesting blogs in advance to start with and commit to posting regularly so you can start to build up a loyal readership. Blogging is a long-term tactic, since it works best with a large audience and strong SEO, which takes time to build.

Podcast

Another option could be to create compelling audio content through establishing your own podcast. Many indie authors adopt this approach that is fast-growing in popularity; back in 2019 there were already 62 million Americans listening to podcasts every week (up 226% since 2013).[33]

This is a great platform to build an audience. If your target audience is readers, then interviewing authors, doing reviews and wrap-ups, and doing readings from your books or other people's books will lend itself more towards readers. If your content is on tips and tricks of writing, then your audience will be other writers. Both are valid strategies. Other writers can be a helpful network to have, because they can help promote your books and you. The downside of podcasts is that they are time consuming and require some degree of technical knowledge.

Community Building

Community building is when you create a group of people to support you. Since they are supporting you, the key to success is gratitude and affection from you. You are asking them to do something for you for free so that you can sell something. You're building a group of people who like you, so you need to make sure that you are likeable. When you are creating a community, you are using relationship marketing, which is you are establishing a kind of 'friendship' with your fans. This means that you need to foster and maintain the community, like you would a friendship. When you're making a friend, you might buy them a cup of coffee. When you're creating a community, the things that you give them are like that cup of coffee.

---

[33] Brad Adgate, 'Podcasting Is Going Mainstream,' *Forbes*, 18 November 2019, www.forbes.com/sites/bradadgate/2019/11/18/podcasting-is-going-mainstream/#7861f8731699

Communities can be created as street teams, Facebook groups or on platforms such as Patreon or Wattpad. When you create these groups, you'll want to consider if the group is for a short-term, task-specific focus or a long-term group. The relationship investment in a short-term group will initially be the same as for a long-term group, but you won't have to maintain the relationship after the task is finished. Street teams are an example of a short term, task-specific group, which can be useful for activities such as promoting your cover reveal or book launch (as mentioned in the previous 'Book Launch Tips' chapter).

Creating a group is time-intensive but can be worth its weight in gold. If you plan on making a career in writing, you'll want to invest in creating a long-term group. They can serve as a source for street teams for book releases or time-limited book promotions. As you grow your community, they become your most loyal readers and will help to promote your books through their recommendations. They can also serve as an additional source of income, if you create a paid membership group.

Whether it's a short-term group or a long-term group, you need to make sure that the members *get something that they want* out of being a member that they couldn't get otherwise. One way to make sure that this happens is to simply ask them, 'What would you like to see?' For some, getting free review copies may be enough. For others, it may be 'swag,' which is branded bookmarks and other limited-edition merchandise. If you're building a long-term group, they may enjoy getting insider information and previews or behind-the-scenes content. In addition to just asking, you can keep track of this by evaluating which approaches get the most attention.

Next, I'll talk about Patreon as an example of a long-term group. The only difference between creating a Patreon community and a Facebook group is the ability to monetise the group. The general mechanics are the same, which are the relationship building and maintaining the activities that you do.

Patreon

Patreon is an online membership platform that allows creators to run a subscription service and earn income by providing regular exclusive content to their patrons. Make sure that you're giving them what they want and not just what's easy for you. This platform may seem quite aspirational for most new writers, but it is worth being aware of as there are a few indie authors who are excellent at using Patreon to cultivate a loyal following and monetise their writing.[34]

You'll also want to create a sense of identity, since this is a long-term group. You've seen YouTubers do this, where they call their fans some kind of nickname. The key to the success of a long-term group is creating a sense that the members belong to some sort of exclusive club, in addition to giving them things that are high quality and highly valued.

Exclusive content could be anything of value to your audience and might include insightful articles, writing advice, tutorial videos, special live sessions, free books, short stories, blogs or podcasts. In addition, you can share sneak peeks of cover reveals and excerpts, which is a great way of getting your potential readers excited about your upcoming releases. Reading people's comments, doing polls and tracking engagement will give you a sense of what the group members are responding to and what you should be providing.

Newsletter

This is a controversial topic, believe it or not. Open rates and click-through rates are often abysmal. Getting people to sign up can be challenging and it's yet another place you have to create content, which can be a lot of work. However, the biggest and best-selling point of newsletters is that you own your mailing list so you can contact people directly. My advice to you is to think of newsletters like 'love letters' to your fans you directly connect with.

> **Top Tip**: Remember to consider what **Call to Action** to incorporate into your newsletter. This simply means what it implies or explicitly requests the audience to do. It is good practice to always include links in newsletters that subscribers can click on (for example to view a sample chapter or download a free novella), so when it's time to click on that 'buy my book' link, they'll be more likely to do so because they're used to clicking on links in your emails.

---

[34] Visit www.patreon.com to learn more about this membership platform that creators can use to run a subscription content service.

Advertising

Advertising is when you pay a platform like social media, a bookseller website or a newspaper to run an advertisement to promote your book. According to Comscore, readers are 64% more likely to purchase a book if they've seen advertising for it beforehand.[35] There are two main forms of advertising: offline and online.

Offline Advertising

This includes all traditional media, such as printed magazines and newspapers, in addition to billboards, posters, television and radio. This type of advertising is generally very expensive, so is usually quite cost prohibitive for indie author budgets. But if you have a very specific target audience in mind it could be worth it, for example a non-fiction book about fishing could be suitable for a national fishing magazine advert.

Online Advertising

This includes all digital channels and incorporates an ever-growing range of options, such as:

- **Direct advertising** on bookseller websites, such as Amazon.
- **Paid promotional listings** on book review websites or newsletters, such as BookBub or Bargain Booksy.
- **Sponsored social media posts** to reach beyond your followers and hashtags.
- **Pay-per-click (PPC) adverts** on search engines, such as Google.
- **Banner adverts** on specific websites.

The main benefits of online advertising are the affordable cost options and the trackability so you can evaluate results. Crucially, most online adverts adopt a pay-per-click (PPC) costing structure so you only pay for the people who have noticed and clicked on your advert. You can also set very specific budgets, for example allocating a $10 spend so when that money is used up then the advert is no longer displayed and you are no

---

[35] 'Make a jaw-dropping book trailer,' *Biteable*, accessed 1 September 2020, www.biteable.com/trailer/book

longer charged. Be aware that Google ads can get really expensive, really fast. Currently, the most economical and effective way to do it is with Facebook ads.

Trackability means that you can measure exactly how many people saw your advert (usually called impressions) and clicked on it, which provides a click-through-rate. For example, if 100 people saw the advert and ten clicked on it, you would have a click-through-rate of 10%. This detailed level of information means that you can analyse what advert content works well and trial different approaches with limited budgets to evaluate impact.

Advertising is a complicated subject to write about with clarity here because there are so many elements to what makes the different types of advertising effective. I have resources on my website to help you with this or you can contact me directly if you have any questions: **www.michelleraabmarketing.com**. My suggestion, though, is to be judicious in your advertising plans. Advertising can become expensive quickly, especially if you don't continually evaluate if it is working to generate sales or not.

Top Tip: There are thousands of helpful resources available to give you insight into different types of advertising. From detailed comparative blog posts, free e-books and step-by-step YouTube tutorial videos – the possibilities are endless. Once you have identified what type of advertising you are interested in, I would recommend researching the topic in more detail to equip yourself with helpful knowledge.

Author Website

While not necessarily a marketing tactic in itself, it probably goes without saying that it is wise to have your own author website. This can act as a hub of information, can help support your other online tactics and can help to establish your credibility as a new author. Plus, this doesn't need to be an expensive venture – in fact it can even be free!

A quick search online will provide you with a plethora of options to explore, including affordable templated versions from companies such as WordPress, in addition to more bespoke websites. I'd advise having a look at other indie author websites to get an idea of what content you could include on yours and asking other writers what they used to create their sites, which provides a good starting point for your research.

Author Profiles on Bookseller Websites and Review Sites

You should always ensure that your author profile is completed on all relevant bookseller websites and review sites, such as Amazon and Goodreads. This helps to present a professional first impression of yourself and may also encourage people to follow you on these channels so they are alerted about your upcoming books.

On the bookseller websites, make sure that your book pages are also fully optimised, such as assigning the book to relevant categories, weaving in relevant search terms into the book description and completing the keyword section. Search for up-to-date information about these topics because they are frequently changing but there are helpful blog articles published every month about keeping on top of these trends.

Publicity

Whereas promotion is when *you* are telling your story, **publicity is when others talk about you**, your books and your brand. Publicity can include exposure in traditional media, such as newspapers, television or radio, as well as being featured on book blogs, websites or bookstagrammer accounts.

Newspapers (printed and online)

Newspapers will only publish stories they see as newsworthy. Newsworthy is whether the story is about something that can impact their readers, is part of the geographical coverage (like a local paper), loss of life or property, or conflict of some kind. They may also tend to publish stories from a particular perspective or with a particular theme, also called angles.

The best way to know what deems a story newsworthy or what angles they tend to write is to read that paper and take notes. Remember to adjust your pitch according to the angle that would be most relevant to the newspaper, such as approaching a city newspaper and saying you were a graduate of the local university that would resonate well with fellow students and local residents.

Podcasters and Bloggers

Treat podcasters and bloggers the same way you would traditional reporters. Find out about their podcast or blog before you pitch them the idea to interview you or to write about your book. For the most part, you don't have to be as formal as with reporters in sending news alerts or press releases, but sending a well-crafted email and attaching your press kit and photos is a must.

Influencer Marketing

This is when an influencer (such as a book blogger, bookstagrammer or celebrity) posts about your book on their platforms. Be warned that bloggers will always share their honest opinion – you can't pay for positive publicity!

Importantly, the influencer is viewed by their audience as a peer; the influencer is just like the audience – they are not an expert or in the media. Their power is from being like their audience and being trusted by their audience.

Whereas a critic is part of the media, an influencer is a reader talking about books they have enjoyed. They have impact because if the influencer likes something and discusses it in a compelling way, their audience will probably like it too. An influencer acts like a friend giving you a recommendation.

The trick with publicity and influencer marketing is for them to tell your story in a positive way, so that the word of mouth advertising that you get is positive. But this can go both ways. If your book is of shoddy quality, then that's the story they will tell, which will quickly damage your reputation. All publicity isn't good, no matter what the adage says.

Pitching a story

Pitching a story is when you try to get a reporter or blogger to cover something about you. Included in the pitch will be your *press kit*. For example, for your local paper the pitch could be that you're a local resident who is doing a reading at your local library.

Press Kit

Your press kit comprises of:

- **Your Press Release**. This should summarise your news story in a way that will resonate with the audience.
- **Your Sales Sheet (or Advanced Information Sheet)**. This should include your book details, author biography and review quotes.
- **High quality photos or videos**.
- **Your contact information**.

You need to ensure that you approach the media *before* the book launch or event. If you are enquiring about if they would be interested in doing a review, send a copy of your e-book or paperback only after they have agreed that they are interested. Unsolicited review copies tend to get automatically binned.

> **Top Tip**: Refer back to the previous 'Book Launch' chapter for more information about creating an Advance Information Sheet, writing a press release and approaching the media.

Word of Mouth

Word of mouth advertising isn't really advertising in the traditional sense because you don't actually pay for it. Instead it is a tactic that promotes your book through other people talking about it. It is the recommendations of friends to friends. Word of mouth is often started by influencers and it's not about the number of followers they have, but about the rapport they have with them. For example, a book blogger may have less than 1,000 followers, but hundreds of those followers might be inclined to buy a book based on their recommendation.

Word of mouth is one of the most powerful forms of promotion in our arsenal, and we have little control over it. The control that we do have is the quality measures that we take to ensure our book and online presence is of a high standard. And of course, you can also approach influencers to enquire if they would be interested in receiving a free copy of your book.

Price

Another key marketing consideration is to ensure that you price your books so they are competitive in the marketplace. Have a look at other titles in your genre, both indie and traditional, to assess what an appropriate price would be for your e-book and paperback.

You'll want to start by doing some research. First, list the books and their prices. You will probably notice a pattern of books that are priced low, medium and high. The lower the price, the faster the book will generally sell, but it may be perceived as having a lower quality. On the other end of the spectrum, the higher the price, the higher the perception that the quality of the book should be excellent. So quick sales versus quality should be one consideration.

Another consideration is if you are well-known or not. If you're a debut author, you may not be able to command a high price. For a price to be competitive, you will want to find the sweet spot between fast sales, perceived quality and your ability to command a certain price. If you set the price too high for the perceived value, readers will walk away.

Specific Campaigns

Specific campaigns are focused on a single goal. Now you have an understanding of basic marketing principles and have been introduced to the range of different tactics you can use, you can start to consider how you might like to incorporate specific promotions throughout the year. These can help to grab the attention of potential readers and generate sales.

What you do is completely up to you and could take the form of a giveaway or a price discount for a limited period. Alternatively, a themed promotion could be creating interesting content to tie in with certain times of the year, such as Christmas or the Summer holiday season.

Timing

When you're planning your marketing activities, you'll need to work out the timing of how everything will fit together. For example, do you want to do lots of activities concurrently for maximum impact (which can work well for an initial book launch) or do you want to drip feed regular activities (which can be helpful to maintain the momentum of sales). You'll also want to balance this with the resources you have available, such as your personal free time and money.

Equally, certain months or events could present good opportunities for targeted promotions. For example, a romance novel could be well received in the run up to Valentine's Day, people may be more receptive to a horror novel around Halloween or a LGBTQ+ novel could be very topical during Pride month.

Remember to be realistic regarding what you have time to prepare and any budget constraints for paid tactics. It is generally more effective to execute a smaller number of promotions really well, rather than attempt to cram in too many that are poorly conceived, which could potentially damage your reputation as an author.

Measuring Success

A vital part of your strategy is how you measure your success. Where having a clear understanding of your story and a clear vision of your brand helps you to focus your marketing strategy and use of tactics, having a way to tell you if you're successful keeps you focused.

If your goal is brand awareness, you want people to know that you exist. One way of learning whether they do is to look at your social media engagement. This is when people take the time to respond to your posts in some way.

If your goal is to know if an advertisement has increased sales, you can evaluate your click-through-rate to analyse how many people clicked on your advert and the figures for how many went on to buy a book.

Measuring your success requires turning your goal into something countable. No matter what your results are, you can use them to tweak and inform future marketing efforts. You can see which kinds of social media or blog posts help more with brand awareness and engagement and which help more with sales.

Your marketing efforts are also cumulative, where each marketing effort builds on your last. To make sure that you're not wandering aimlessly in the wilderness, I recommend that you keep track of your marketing efforts so you can ensure you get the most out of them. Your money and your time are precious, so you want to make sure that you're spending both in the most efficient way possible.

Creating Your Marketing Plan

Hopefully this chapter has provided you with enough information to start coming up with your own marketing plan. Remember to do your research when it comes to exploring the more technical aspects of the various tactics you want to adopt. The advice surrounding a lot of these areas is forever changing, but there are ample resources for you to consult. These range from free blogs, online articles and downloadable examples, to author marketing books, courses or even hiring a professional to help you out if you feel overwhelmed.

Just to recap, the main components that make up your marketing plan are as follows:

- **Strategy**: *why* you are choosing certain goals.
- **Target Audience**: *who* are your potential readers.
- **Goals**: *what* you want to achieve.
- **Tactics**: *how* to achieve those goals.
- **Pricing**: *how much* your books cost.
- **Specific Campaigns**: *which* specific promotions are planned.
- **Timing**: *when* will everything happen.
- **Measures**: *how you will know* if activities have been successful.

You can do this. You've done the hardest part already – you've written a book! Marketing is just making sure that your book baby gets all the love it deserves.

Sample Marketing Plan

Strategy: Target purchasing intent stage 2 (reader deciding which book to purchase).

Goal: Get reader to choose your book to purchase.

Tactic: Do a giveaway of your first few chapters on your website.

Implementation: Leading up to the giveaway publish blog posts about the process of creating this giveaway. On your newsletter, announce the upcoming giveaway. You can reuse the text from the blog posts for this and social media posts by breaking it into smaller chunks and tweak it a little so that each chunk stands alone.

Then, make the first few chapters of your book available on your website for download (or on Wattpad or on Patreon). During the giveaway, post about it a few times or more a week. Have a call to action like requiring their email address for download. Run an ad on Facebook about the giveaway before and during the giveaway period.

Measures: Use a separate bitly link (or similar) for each of your ads, blog posts, newsletters and social media posts for the sample download, to provide precise measurements of where your downloads originated from. At the end, you'll be able to see which platform got you the most downloads.

About the Author
Michelle Raab

Dr. Michelle Raab holds a doctorate in psychology, specialising in quantitative psychology. She runs Michelle Raab Marketing which provides personalised branding and marketing solutions for indie authors and other businesses. She is known for her dedication to her clients, her creativity and her science-informed knowledge. She has a knack for helping clients gain clarity and create the best marketing plan for them.

Michelle is currently writing a sci-fi story that she plans to self-publish. She is the founder and leader of the indie creative community World Indie Warriors, which is dedicated to uplifting and supporting indie creatives. Her most important job, though, is being a mum.

Visit **https://bit.ly/michellemail** to join the Michelle Raab Marketing community and receive tips and exclusive offers.

Connect Online
- **Websites:**
    - o www.michelleraabmarketing.com
    - o www.michelleraabwrites.com
    - o www.worldindiewarriors.org
- **Facebook:**
    - o www.facebook.com/michelleraabmarketing
    - o www.facebook.com/michelleraabwrites
    - o www.facebook.com/worldindiewarriors
- **Instagram:**
    - o @michelleraabmarketing
    - o @michelleraabwrites
    - o @worldindiewarriors

Writing Community
by Holly Lyne

It's All About Making Friends and Influencing People

It's often said that writing can be a solitary profession. When done a certain way, that's absolutely true. But I've actually found it to be quite the opposite.

I've been independently publishing since 2013. That's how long I've been taking this at least somewhat seriously. While much of the actual writing does happen with no one else physically present (except for my family), I've never felt more part of a community in my life.

I've cultivated online friendships with people from all over the world. We're all different, we write in a variety of genres, we're of all ages and backgrounds, we all have our own processes and yet we are all connected through our love of writing. In fact, these days most of my friends are other authors. While I have maintained a few other friendships, more and more I'm choosing to spend my time with writers, both virtually and in person. With a very small number of exceptions, the indie author community is welcoming, inclusive and incredibly supportive.

Where Do You Find These People?

There are writers everywhere and there are lots of ways to find them. A number of my writer friendships began in Facebook groups, many more on Instagram. There is a group of local authors who I initially connected with on Facebook, but who I meet up with for drinks and cake a few times a year. In December we have a meal out together and joke that it is our equivalent of an office Christmas party.

There are local writers' circles and critique groups or you can meet other authors at conferences, events and writing courses. There is virtually no end to the means of connecting with other writers.

> **Top Tip**: I highly recommend joining the Alliance of Independent Authors (ALLi). There is a fee to join, but in return you get a whole host of member discounts and benefits, and access to an incredible network of hard-working and highly successful indie authors to learn from and connect with. You can find out more here: **www.allianceindependentauthors.org**

Ways of connecting with other authors:

- **Local writing groups**: Check out your local community centre and library, or search on social media for groups in your area.
- **Facebook groups**: You can discover a growing range of Facebook groups by searching 'writing group' or 'writers' etc. Examples include World Indie Warriors, Unstoppable Authors and Rebel Authors.
- **Websites to connect with other writers**: Some sites offer free trials, others are paid subscriptions, but they could be worth it to make meaningful connections. Examples include Scribophile and Inked Voices.
- **Writing retreats**: Going on a retreat provides you with valuable time to focus on your craft and bond with like-minded individuals who totally get you.
- **Writing conferences, literary festivals or workshops**: There are a wide range of writing events that take place in every country, typically on an annual basis.
- **National Novel Writing Month (NaNoWriMo)**: Participating in the annual NaNoWriMo event not only encourages you to start writing, but their member forums are a great way to connect with others.[36] Plus, using the relevant hashtags on social media can connect you with participants from all over the world.
- **Join different writers' associations**: These communities are genuinely committed to supporting the career development of their members by assisting them in increasing their industry knowledge and honing their craft. Examples include The Alliance of Independent Authors and associations for specific genres, such as The Crime Writers' Association.

---

[36] Visit www.nanowrimo.org to learn more about this non-profit organisation that provides free tools, community connections and events to help all writers finish their novels.

- **Online search**: You can discover writing groups by location by searching online or using websites such as **www.meetup.com.**
- **Social media**: This provides a plethora of options to connect with like-minded authors. There are also numerous writing challenges and author follow loops you can take part in to discover other writers.
- **Start your own writing group**: If there are no writers' groups in your area that appeal to you, there is always the option to create your own group and make it exactly what you want it to be.

Talk It Out

One of my favourite means of connecting over the last year or so, is through podcasting. In early 2019, I suggested to one of my writing friends, Angeline Trevena (the author of the earlier 'Worldbuilding' chapter) that we resurrect her old podcast and relaunch it as a two-woman show. And so *Unstoppable Authors*[37] was born. We've been through a rebrand since then (it was originally *The Great Western Woods Worldbuilding Podcast*) and began interviewing guests in September 2019. I've had the opportunity to speak on other people's podcasts as well and have made some excellent friends through this process. There's really very little substitute when it comes to connecting with people than by actually talking with them, asking and answering questions and really getting to know them.

When you pick the brains of a writer who is doing something different and having success that you aspire to, you can learn so much. If you choose to go into podcasting and interviewing authors, never be afraid to pitch to the people ahead of you on the road. I've never been turned down yet. As long as you're respectful, acknowledge the value of their time, make it clear that you're familiar with their body of work and what they can offer your listeners, then they are unlikely to say no. The same goes for pitching yourself to appear as a guest on someone else's podcast. Make sure their show is relevant, that they do actually interview people, you've got something to offer their listeners and you shine in your pitch.

Unstoppable Authors isn't just a passive experience either. We are active on Patreon, where supporters of the show get access to behind-the-scenes content and an even deeper sense of connection with us. In addition, we

---

[37] Visit www.unstoppableauthors.wordpress.com to find out more about our podcast, worldbuilding course and upcoming events.

have a lively Facebook group and an Instagram account where we run challenges, have discussions and share the journey with writers all over the world. We are all unstoppable authors and our community is all about that tenacity.

When podcasting, every now and then you'll chat with someone who you connect with more deeply and a friendship will form. Those friendships can be absolutely invaluable. For instance, I interviewed one guest, Daniel Willcocks, which then turned into him interviewing both Angeline and I. We kept in touch and now I'm working with Dan on his *Great Writers Share* podcast as well.[38] You never know what will flourish from one conversation.

One Thing Leads to Another...

Since we began podcasting, Angeline and I have come up with a number of collaborative ideas: we launched a worldbuilding course, built a world together to write in and planned our very own writing conference, *Indie Fire*. We sadly had to postpone the first event, which was meant to take place in May 2020 during the global COVID-19 pandemic and associated UK lockdown. But we're still determined to make it happen once the world rights itself.

---

[38] Visit www.danielwillcocks.com/greatwritersshare to learn more about the podcast and the Patreon community, including how to join the private Slack group.

Indie Fire is an event focused on indie authors, with numerous workshops and panel discussions featuring successful self-published authors who will share what they have learned along the way to where they are now. It's about bringing writers from around the UK together to share ideas, knowledge and to make connections.

It will also incorporate a book market providing writers with the opportunity to sell their books and chat to readers. For up-to-date information about upcoming events visit **www.indiefire.uk.**

Writing conferences are a fantastic way to not only develop your writing craft and marketing skills, but to connect with other writers. Lots of them! There's something special about the community coming together to share ideas. It's genuinely so inspiring. We can all learn so much from each other and in a group setting like that it's even more potent.

There is this energy in the room from all of those minds being alert and receptive. The questions get everyone thinking. The discussion sparks other ideas and before you know it, you're coming away with all the plans. You just might make a connection at an event that will turn out to be pivotal for your career.

It's About Who You Know

Like with a lot of other industries, in the indie publishing world it can make a big difference to your success if you know the right people. Being interviewed on one of the popular podcasts, signing up with a small press or being able to secure a big name to review your book can propel you to dizzying new heights of success.

Success is, of course, in the eye of the beholder. Maybe there is no appeal in rubbing shoulders with famous folks or making seven figure sales.

Perhaps success is measured in time free to be with your family or simply finishing that book. But regardless of what your definition of success is, the writing community can be there to support you.

When you connect with authors from different walks of life, you can be opened up to lots of learning opportunities too. If you're a new author who is self-publishing for the first time, there is so much to be learned from those who have gone through the process before and can share their expertise.

Create New Opportunities to Reach More Readers

People may be genuinely interested in reading your books, especially if you connect with authors who write (and read) in a similar genre to you. Most writers are also avid readers and they understand the value of a review or recommendation, so are more likely to become cheerleaders for your book if they really enjoy it.

Your fellow authors can be the best source of superfans that you'll find anywhere and they can help to promote your book to their audiences, so you'll reach more readers than you might on your own.

This might be in the form of:

- **Joint/group promotions** through sites like BookFunnel.
- **Newsletter swaps**, which can be organised in specialised Facebook groups.
- **Including another author's book blurb** in the back of your own (and them reciprocating).

The Practical Things

Your writer network can also help with practical things, such as providing feedback on your cover design or sharing insights on what type of advertising works for different genres.

It's also useful to connect with others in order to exchange recommendations, for example on editing, cover design and book promotion services. This gives you insight not just into how good the service providers are at their job but also what they are really like to work with. It can help you avoid scams and assess what is good value for money.

Top Tip: There may be opportunities to give back and help other writers, which in turn can generate interest in your own works – a win-win situation. For example, when I launched my debut non-fiction book, *Goal Setting for Writers*, I was invited to lead an online workshop hosted by the World Indie Warriors writing community. This was a wonderful promotional opportunity for my book and it also allowed me to connect with more lovely writers.

Find Beta Readers or Critique Partners

Connecting with members of the writing community can be a good way of finding beta readers or critique partners to give honest opinions on your books. This is generally better than relying on friends and family who may not want to be too harsh and hurt your feelings.

Other writers can be encouraging, supportive and uplifting while providing useful, constructive criticism, which can in turn help you to improve your writing. You may also have the opportunity to do the same for others and it can be hugely exciting to be involved in shaping a book.

But It's Also the Little Things That Matter the Most

For writers who would prefer not to always work alone, there are groups all over the internet for sharing goals, doing writing sprints and seeking support. Livestream sprinting sessions are where I get the bulk of my words done these days. Someone will host a livestream on YouTube, Facebook or Instagram; they start a timer and everyone writes with total focus for a short burst of time. When the time is up, everyone shares their word-count. The competitive side of me loves trying to beat someone else or just improve upon my own previous score. It's usually a good laugh too.

Angeline and I host livestreams in our Facebook group for *Unstoppable Authors*. We sometimes invite guests to chat in between sprints. There may occasionally be alcohol involved! This type of community writing time can be extremely productive. Whether it's the camaraderie, competition or just that little bit of pressure to focus during the sprints, something makes this time extra wordy for me and many others.

Another way of doing word sprints with others is in chat groups. Rather than anyone being on camera and broadcasting, you just jump into a relevant group and see if anyone else is around to do sprints with.

Over on the *Great Writers Share* we have a Slack group for our patrons and have a sprint channel where a bunch of us do sprints most days. I'm writing these very words during a sprint session with my co-hosts, as it happens.

In addition, I'm a member of several Discord servers that have sprint channels that I've used in the past. You can also set up a group of writing friends in Facebook Messenger, WhatsApp or Instagram chat and do sprints there.

Of course, you can do sprints on your own, but why not try out writing along with others and enjoy the feeling of being cheered on and the accountability of having to share your wordcount? You don't have to be in this on your own. Find your people and write with them.

Be Accountable

One of my favourite things about the writing community is the accountability. In the *Unstoppable Authors* Facebook group, we do weekly and monthly accountability posts where we share our goals and our progress towards them. This is a big part of how I get done as much as I do. It's why I gave this topic a chapter of its own in my book, *Goal Setting for Writers*.

There's nothing quite like putting your goals out there for others to see to make you actually commit to progressing them. Writers will understand like no one else just how important your wordcount is to you. It encourages you to prioritise your writing and carve out time for it when life might otherwise be a barrier. It's harder to procrastinate if you've got a group of fellow writers waiting to hear how you're getting on.

Research shows that when you write down your goals and share them with other people, you are far more likely to achieve them. The psychology of why is a bit beyond the scope of this chapter, but needless to say it works. So, join an accountability group, share your goals and support your fellow writers in theirs. You may be surprised how far it takes you.

Collaborate, Baby!

One of the other opportunities that can come along when you engage with the writing community is the chance to participate in multi-author anthologies or collections. This can be a bit of a mixed bag, so tread carefully. Make sure you collaborate with the right people and that the opportunity is the right one for where you are in your journey.

I've been involved in two fiction anthologies so far and I've learnt a lot from both. When you work with other writers to publish something you will almost always learn some dos and don'ts. They can offer you the chance to get in front of new readers, grow your own mailing list or social media following, connect you with other writers in your genre and generate a good income. But make sure that you understand the brief and your rights. It's likely you'll be giving up the copyright to your contribution, at least for a short time. Make sure there is a contract involved and that you fully understand what you are signing up to.

The first anthology I participated in was a combination of ten authors' first-in-series books that were already published. I didn't need to write anything new, just join in with promoting it and watch the royalties roll in.

The second was a series of short story anthologies, the *Magic Underground* series. This was a bigger undertaking. There were over twenty authors involved initially and we each had to write three brand new short stories. But this second opportunity came about as a direct result of the first, as it was the same organiser who invited me to participate.

There are a whole host of options out there for anthologies if it is something you're interested in. You can keep an eye out for small presses taking submissions, you can club together with your writer friends or organise one yourself. It can be a lot of work, but also incredibly rewarding. Hopefully it will be a fun and interesting experience if you try it.

Share the Words

The other form of collaboration that might come your way once you're deeply involved in the author community is the opportunity to co-write with another writer. Books like this one, with multiple contributors each doing their own thing, is one form of co-writing.

But people do write fiction together, with each writer bringing their own strengths to the project. Some partnerships work with one writer creating the plan or first draft, with another giving it a more finished flare. Others plot out the story together and both dig in and write the first draft. There are as many ways to co-write as there are partnerships.

Again, you'll want to make sure that all parties are clear on their role, have a contract and plan for how to split any expenses and profits between you. I highly recommend checking out *Collaboration for Authors* by Daniel Willcocks if this is an area you want to explore in more depth.

Friends with Benefits

The indie author community is a close knit one. We all support one another in a lot of ways. By building genuine friendships with other writers you might benefit from discounted prices (or 'mate's rates') if they also provide other services, such as editing, book cover design or interior formatting. I've certainly benefited from this perk, with friends providing heavily discounted covers and formatting.

Be tactful though – being offered a generous discount is one thing, demanding one is quite another – as is the blatant expectation that people would provide you something for free just because they know you. Be respectful that this is their livelihood. Just as you wouldn't expect your friends to give you free copies of their books as you would want to purchase a copy in order to show your support, the same is true for any services they may offer. We can all help each other out by paying a fair price and recommending them to others.

We've Got Your Back

All in all, the writing community is supportive, sociable and the perfect antidote to that old stereotype about writing always being a solitary pursuit. We're on a shared journey, even though we each take our own route. We understand the struggles and the joys of choosing this path. There is no need to sit alone wondering if you're getting it right. Get involved in the community and you'll soon see that we all ask ourselves that and there is only one true answer: there is no right way!

It can be daunting to be a new writer. It's a steep learning curve and there is so much information out there that it can be a struggle to sift through it. Your writer friends can help to filter through it all and break down the overwhelm.

Being connected to other writers can provide motivation, inspiration and support. This can build your confidence and self-esteem, and, of course, lead to genuine, long-lasting friendships.

About the Author
Holly Lyne

Holly Lyne is an urban fantasy author, podcaster and bullet journal enthusiast with a knack for organisation and getting stuff done.

She lives in Yorkshire with her husbeast, two children and midwife cat. When not juggling family commitments, she writes dark urban fantasy novels, purging her imagination of its demons. Inspired by the King of Horror himself, Holly aspires to be at least half as prolific and successful and promises to limit herself to only one tome of *The Stand*-like proportions in her career.

She has released nine novels as H.B. Lyne, including the *Shifters of Caerton* series, the *Lies the Dead Tell* series and *The Hidden City* series (part of the *Magic Underground* anthology). She has also released a non-fiction book as Holly Lyne: *Goal Setting for Writers: A Step-by-Step Roadmap to Success* .

Connect Online
- **Website:** www.hblyne.com
- **Instagram:** @hblyne
- **Facebook:** www.facebook.com/authorhblyne
- **Unstoppable Authors Podcast:** www.unstoppableauthors.com
- **Unstoppable Authors Patreon:** patreon.com/unstoppableauthors
- **Great Writers Share Podcast:** pod.link/1473869415
- **Great Writers Share Patreon:** www.patreon.com/greatwritersshare

Bookstagram
by Marie Landry

Entering the World of Bookstagram

To be a successful author these days, you need a social media presence. Not only does it help readers find you and your books, it's also the best way to build a connection with readers (and fellow writers).

Instagram is a particularly helpful platform. With millions of people using the app daily, that's millions of potential readers at your fingertips. Social media is incredibly fast-paced, but it's been proven that posts with pictures get more attention, making Instagram the perfect outlet for authors to grab readers' attention by creating compelling content – something we're doing anyway.

As a writer, whether you're published yet or not, it's always wise to connect with existing book bloggers and bookstagrammers (see the previous Book Launch chapter for advice regarding making these connections).

Instagram can be a useful tool, no matter how you choose to use it, but you may find you want to take it a step further and join the world of bookstagram.

What is Bookstagram and How Does it Differ from a Regular Instagram Account?

So, you're a writer who wants to enter the wonderful world of bookstagramming on Instagram. One of the first things you need to know is that there's a difference between having an author account and being a bookstagrammer. Both have merit and should always be set up as a public account so your readers can find you, which may require setting up a separate profile from your personal account if you want to keep some posts about your life private. Your decision about what type of account to pursue will depend on your personal style of photography, how much time you want to dedicate to the platform and whether you're as much of a reader as you are a writer.

An **author account** is typically more of a personal account where the focus is on the author and *their* books. There's usually a mix of promotional posts about their books and some 'real life' posts featuring anything from family and pets to travel and hobbies. A **bookstagram account** is a dedicated bookish account that's typically more curated and stylised and features a wide range of books by various authors.

Bookstagram is for you if:

- You want to promote your own books in a more casual way where they are not the main focus of your account.
- You enjoy promoting other authors, books and publishers.
- You enjoy photography.
- You are looking for a fun creative outlet.

My Experience as a Bookstagrammer

With a dozen self-published books released over a span of nearly nine years, I've been on every social media platform imaginable. Starting a bookstagram account four years ago was one of the smartest moves I've ever made, and it's proven to be an invaluable tool.

Through bookstagram, I've made connections with readers and writers all over the world. I've successfully launched books, I've helped countless authors and it's proven to be my favourite creative outlet next to writing.

In this chapter, I'll explain how to help a novice Instagrammer set up a compelling bookstagram account if this is the direction you wish to take for your author social media presence.

Getting Started

What to Post on Your Bookstagram

I always think of bookstagram as *all books, all the time*. There is no right or wrong, and there are as many styles as there are bookstagrammers. Some prefer simple pictures that let the books speak for themselves, while others use all kinds of props to enhance their photos.

As for the actual books to post, you can share your favourite books, the books you buy, what you're currently reading, your bookshelves, you holding a book – the possibilities are endless! We'll get into posting about your own books specifically later on.

Props

Not sure what kinds of props to use? I've been bookstagramming for so long that I now see just about anything as a potential prop. Look at other bookstagrammers' accounts for ideas and inspiration if you need some guidance. Simply search on Instagram using bookish hashtags, such as #bookstagram, to find a huge range of accounts.

If you don't want to spend much, or any, money on props, take a look around your home and see what you have that could work, or get outside if you can and use nature or interesting architecture as your backdrop.

Some examples of props:

- Candles
- Blankets
- Scarves, sweaters or jackets
- Mugs
- Bookmarks
- Book sleeves
- Flowers (real or artificial)
- Funko Pops, figurines or other collectibles
- Other books

Choosing the Right Equipment

You don't need fancy camera equipment for bookstagram. Most smartphones are equipped with incredible cameras, which are more than good enough for your purposes. It's a dream of mine to someday own a DSLR camera, but I currently take 100% of my pictures on my Samsung phone.

The key to any good picture, regardless of how you're taking it, is good lighting. Natural light is always best, but you can also buy lights online that are helpful for indoor photography. Over the years, I've learned to utilise sunny days for photoshoots and I get my setup as close to a window as possible.

Editing Your Photos

Instagram has built-in editing software and filters that work well, especially for newer bookstagrammers as they find a style that works for them. With the built-in editing, you can adjust brightness, contrast, sharpness and add filters, although I always suggest using those sparingly unless you use the same filter for every photo.

There is a plethora of photo-editing apps you can download on your phone or desktop, and many of them are free. Some of the best-known ones are Lightroom, VSCO and Snapseed. I've been using the mobile version of Lightroom exclusively for several years and I highly recommend it. I always joke that it's like a magic wand; you can take any picture, even one that was taken in poor lighting, and vastly improve it with a few clicks of a button. There are many photographers, bloggers and bookstagrammers who offer Lightroom tutorials and even free presets that you can download and save to the app. I've created my own preset that I use on every single one of my pictures to create a cohesive look within my feed. The way my photos are edited, along with my own personal style, makes my photos instantly recognisable.

Using Your Voice

An interesting picture is what will catch a viewer's eye and draw them in, but you want them to stick around and hopefully even follow you. That's where a compelling caption comes in.

A caption is the best way to give people an idea of your voice. Are you funny? Do you want to inspire people? Do you want to spread awareness about something? Do you want to be known for something specific?

For example, I have a casual, humorous writing style on bookstagram, which ties in well with the writing style I use in my books. I talk about a variety of things; from the novels I'm reading to what I'm watching on TV and what I'm writing. I tell anecdotes about my day or something that happened in the past that ties in with the picture I'm posting. I'm also a mental health advocate and I speak openly and often about my struggles with mental health, the importance of self-care and I do regular 'check-ins' with my audience. I try to post content that is relatable because it makes people feel like they're part of my story or like we're friends who are having a chat. Give people an inside view of the person behind the photo and they're more likely to connect with you and stick around.

By writing compelling captions, you can keep your audience coming back for more. They'll be curious about what you have to say, even if you talk about a variety of topics.

You should also create a captivating bio for your account. You have 150 characters to give people an idea of who you are, so you need to use that space wisely. Go beyond the facts and add some flair to your bio.

Some suggestions:

- Mention the genre you read and/or write.
- Is there something about you that you consider a fun fact?
- Do you collect anything?
- Short, punchy statements work well and give a glimpse into your personality; for example, 'fuelled by coffee,' 'sci-fi movie aficionado,' or 'lover of rock n' roll.'
- Some people also mention the fandoms they belong to, which gives other people something to connect to instantly; 'Sherlocked,' 'Whovian,' or 'Star Wars fan,' that sort of thing.

Incorporating e-books

Many readers these days read exclusively on an e-reader, and some self-published authors only have books available in an e-book format. It's up to you whether you post only physical books, only e-books or a mix. However, if you're posting pictures of e-books, you should be aware that photographing e-books can be tricky. There is often a glare on the screen, which means you need to get the angle and the lighting just right. You might have to play around with this until you find something that works.

Top Tip: After years of dealing with glares and reflections while photographing e-books, I've started photoshopping covers onto my e-reader. I set up my shot, take a picture with the e-reader turned off, open the photo in Adobe Photoshop and superimpose the cover onto the ereader. If you don't have Photoshop software, there are websites such as Pixlr and Canva that will allow you to do this. If you need help, a simple Google search will garner plenty of results.

Developing Your Style

Creating a Cohesive Feed

Decide whether you want to have a theme or not for your bookstagram account. A theme can be anything from using the same set of props and maintaining a specific editing style to using the same basic layout or colour scheme. If you decide to have a theme, be sure to keep it consistent, but don't be afraid to change things up from time to time. I tend to change my themes seasonally, using different props and a different preset filter/lighting.

Pick a specific spot or two where you take most of your photos. For example, the natural light is best in my bedroom/office, so I have two main spots where I do photoshoots: a small table with a white background for flatlay photos, and my bed with cushions in the background for book stacks.

You should also consider:

- Do you want to do all flatlays, all book stacks or a mixture?
- Do you want to take all of your pictures indoors, outdoors or have a mix? If you have a mix, this is where a consistent editing style will keep your feed looking cohesive.
- Are you photogenic? Do you enjoy being in front of the camera as much as being behind it? Get in the shot! There are some bookstagrammers who are in every single one of their own pictures, either facing the camera, with their back to it or pictures taken from above with just their legs or feet in the shot.

> **Top Tip**: Having a cohesive feed doesn't mean you need to pigeon-hole yourself. I post a wide variety of content, including flatlays, book stacks, pictures with me in them and pictures with different props, but my editing style keeps it looking cohesive, regardless of what I post. Creating cohesion within your feed will take some forethought, planning and maybe even some trial and error.

Being Original and Showing Your Personality

Imitation is *not* the highest form of flattery! Don't copy other booksta-grammers. With that being said, keep in mind there is a difference between *imitation* and *inspiration*. I get inspired by fellow bookstagrammers on a daily basis. There are so many creative, talented people in the bookish commu-nity who blow me away with their originality. If you'd like to try something similar to what someone else has done, be sure to put your own unique spin on it. Let your creativity and your personality shine!

Being original helps differentiate your account from others. I said earlier that my photos are instantly recognisable because of the props I use and my editing style, but it's also partly because I have a 'mascot' of sorts: a little felt fox who appears in all of my pictures. I'm also an unapologetic nerd and you can often find fandom-themed photos in my feed, showcas-ing anything from *Star Wars* and *Doctor Who* to *Disney*.

Considering Your Audience

Building Relationships with Other Bookstagrammers

There are a number of important things to keep in mind as you begin building relationships. **Authenticity is key.** Some people join Instagram looking to gain fame, influence and legions of followers and fans. You should be on bookstagram because you *want* to be, you want to connect with other people and you have a genuine love of books (not just your own!)

The Don'ts:

- Don't slide into people's direct messages (DMs) or comments promoting yourself or begging people to read your book.
- Don't randomly comment on people's posts promoting yourself.
- Sometimes people will ask for specific recommendations and if your book fits the bill, feel free to mention it. Otherwise, don't try to sell yourself to people. It feels fake and pushy and is likely to turn potential readers off.
- Don't go into it expecting something in return; befriending people on bookstagram isn't a guarantee they'll read your book.
- Posting about other author's books doesn't mean they owe you anything in return.

Bookstagram should be about sharing your love of books without expectation of favours or rewards of any kind. This is a long game and you'll need to be patient. You won't get thousands of followers overnight. Building relationships, and building trust with your audience, takes time and you need to do it in a natural way. The payoff is worth it though; you'll meet people from all over the world, make new friends, find fellow writers to connect with and gain people's trust by being your authentic self, which in turn makes it easier to sell books.

Interacting with Your Followers

One of the best ways to encourage engagement with your followers is by asking a question in your caption. You can relate your question to your caption or to the picture itself. For example, if you're talking about a book with a certain trope, ask readers for their favourite books that employ that trope. If your caption is more general and not necessarily related to your photo that day, include your audience by asking for their opinion or by inviting them to share a story similar to yours.

When people comment on your posts, be sure to respond. If their response leaves you curious about something, ask a follow-up question and try to get a dialogue going. Similarly, when people DM you, be sure to reply.

Leave meaningful comments on other people's posts. People often visit the profiles of those who have commented on their posts to return the favour, so this is a great way to expand your following and meet new people. Just make sure you're being genuine and your comments are more than generic things like, 'nice pic' or 'great post.'

Genre

Keep your own genre in mind when creating content. Many authors write in one genre while having eclectic reading tastes, but it would help to stick mostly to your own genre for the purposes of bookstagram. For example, as a romance author, my target audience is obviously romance readers. If I posted mostly about fantasy or horror books, it would send mixed messages and confuse potential new followers.

People like to know what to expect when they follow you; the first few rows of photos in your profile will give them an idea of the types of books you post about, so make sure it's easy to tell at a glance. That's not to say you can never post about other genres; while my feed is mostly romance books, I do occasionally share books in other genres.

People will follow you for book recommendations, so if you regularly recommend books in your own genre, they'll likely be more receptive when you're promoting your own work.

Picking the Right Posting Time and Frequency

There have been various studies done about the optimal time of day to post, but I think ultimately it depends on what works best for you. Some people will want to post first thing in the morning before the day gets busy, some will squeeze in a post during a break and some will post in the evenings during downtime. If you have the freedom to post at any time during the day, experiment with different times and see if one seems to get more traction and then try to stick with that.

One big thing to take into consideration is where the majority of your audience is from. My time zone is EST and the majority of my followers live in Canada and the United States, with a fair number in the UK. That means all Canadian and American time zones are within three hours behind or one hour ahead of me. The UK is five hours ahead, with Europe an hour ahead of that. I typically post between 10 and 11am, which means the majority of my followers are likely awake if they live in a time zone that's behind mine, while people in the UK are well into their day. Posting in the morning has the added benefit of seeing likes and comments trickle in throughout the day and it gives me a chance to visit other bookstagrammers' profiles sporadically throughout the day.

More important than the time you post is the frequency of your posts. **Consistency is key**. Consistency will mean something different for everyone, depending on their schedule, but in my experience, I get more engagement when I post daily or nearly every day. You might not have time, enough content or enough to say to post daily and that's fine, but try to post at least a few times a week if you're able to.

You can of course prepare content in advance and schedule when to post it in the future. It is often more time-efficient to take a batch of bookstagram photos at the same time, especially if you are using similar props or layouts.

Diversity in Bookstagram

Consider the types of books you're sharing or want to share. Are the authors all white? All straight or cis-gender? Bookstagram is a fantastic place to showcase books by a variety of authors from every walk of life. For example, if all the books you read are by white authors, consider diversifying your shelves and adding in some different representation.

You can, and should, post diverse books all year, but there are certain events that present the perfect opportunity for tie-ins, such as rainbow book stacks or books that highlight LGBTQ+ authors and stories during Pride Month (June), books by and about black authors during Black History Month (February) and books by and about Jewish authors during Hanukkah.

Growing Your Account

Using Hashtags Strategically

Next to being an active member of the community and engaging with other bookstagrammers, hashtags are one of the most effective tools to get your pictures seen. Users can discover content by searching for or following specific hashtags, which can extend your reach beyond your followers. Think of them as keywords for a search engine, albeit confined to Instagram posts.

You can use up to 30 hashtags per post. The key is to use them strategically; just because you can use 30 doesn't necessarily mean you *should*, especially if you're not using relevant hashtags.

In order for hashtags to be effective, you want to use ones that are popular but not too popular, and you want to mix them up a bit for each post. If you use the exact same set of hashtags on every post, it might flag Instagram's spam sensors and temporarily block your account.

To see how many times a hashtag has been used, type it into the search bar on Instagram and the number of photos will show up. For my own posts, I have a list of hashtags I use consistently, which include approximately 10 hashtags with 10,000-100,000 hits and another 10 with 100,000-500,000 hits. I also add hashtags that are relevant to the content of the picture itself, whether it's genre-specific, the author's name, the name of the publisher or the type of picture, such as flatlay, book stack or outdoor shot. As a general rule, I try not to use hashtags with over one million hits because then the photo gets buried almost immediately by other posts and won't be seen. Similarly, you don't want to use too many hashtags with only a few hundred hits because not many people will see your post.

How Do You Find Hashtags?

One of the best ways I've found to discover hashtags is to check out bookstagrammers and authors who post content similar to mine and see what they are using. You can also find hashtags within the search function on Instagram; when you type in a hashtag and click on it, there will usually be a list of similar hashtags that are popular among users. You can also partially type in a hashtag to check out the autocomplete options, which may give you more ideas.

Alternative strategies to discover bookish hashtags include searching for online articles about the latest bookstagram trends, exploring the large number of freely available online Instagram Hashtag Generator tools or using dedicated apps, such as Smarthash, InstaTag, AutoHash, Top Tags and Hashme.

> **Top Tip**: You should also regularly check the up-to-date online lists that outline which hashtags have been permanently or temporarily banned because they do not meet Instagram's community guidelines. Using banned hashtags could block, penalise or shadowban your account, which means that all your posts become limited so only your followers can see them and all your other hashtags will stop working to bring up your content in search results. One of the seemingly innocent hashtags that is currently banned is #books – never use that one.[39]

Join an Event

If you need a creative boost or some inspiration, **join some bookstagram challenges**. Many bookstagrammers host monthly challenges for the community with daily prompts. You don't need to participate every day, but these challenges can help get the creative juices flowing, plus it's a great way to find other bookstagrammers.

You could also **join a readathon**. Some readathons last for a weekend, some for a week, some for a month. Some are for a specific book or series, while others have a theme, such as holiday books in December, LGBTQ+ books during Pride Month or seasonal books during the appropriate season. Others simply encourage you to read as much as you can of any book you want during the readathon time frame.

Finally, you could **participate in a #StackForACause challenge**. These are created from time to time by bookstagrammers who want to raise awareness, and often money, for a cause. For example, in May during Mental Health Awareness Month, a group of bookstagrammers regularly encourage readers to post a green book stack and use a specific hashtag. For every book stack shared using the challenge's hashtag, the group donate $2 to a mental health initiative. This is a great way to support different causes and it's also useful to meet other bookstagrammers who care about the same things.

---

[39] Cheslea Evans, 'Banned Instagram Hashtags 2020 - Tags You Didn't Know Were Blocked,' *Markitors*, 2 January 2020, https://markitors.com/banned-instagram-hashtags

Using Stories

Stories are posts that last for 24 hours and show up at the top of Instagram when you open the app. They're perfect for sharing less curated pictures, snippets of life, what you're reading and information about your writing.

Stories have a lot of fun features you can play around with. You can record videos, either of yourself speaking to your audience or of things that work better in video format than photo form. For example, you could tell a funny story, read a snippet from your work-in-progress or newest release, give a tour of your bookshelves, add emojis and gifs to text, ask a question or create a poll, and so many other things. All of these are ways for fellow bookstagrammers to get to know you in a more casual way.

You can also share other people's content. If you see a post you really like and want to spread the love, you can click on the little icon under the photo that looks like a paper airplane, then click on 'add post to your story' and it will appear in your stories. Tag the creator of the original post so they know you enjoy their content. Some people also do 'Follow Friday' or 'Shout-out Saturday' features where they tag accounts or post specific pictures they've been enjoying recently.

Top Tip: If you want to keep your stories, you can create 'Highlights' that stay on your profile indefinitely. You can create categories for your highlights to keep things neat and to help viewers find specific content. For example, whenever I post about my writing in my stories, I add it to a highlight I created called 'Writer Life'. If I'm talking about fandom things or what I'm currently watching and loving, I'll add it to my 'Fangirl' highlight. I also keep reading updates, information about my published books and much more.

Promoting Your Books

Striking the Right Balance

There will be times when you'll likely switch from casually posting your book here and there to having it at the forefront of your account, like during a cover reveal, sale or new release, and that's fine. Use your bookstagram however you see fit and don't be afraid to use it as a promotional tool when it feels right.

Casually include your book whenever it feels natural. If you're posting a blue book stack and your book has a blue spine, include it. If you're posting about a certain trope or a specific type of character, that hits your book, include it. The subtlety of posting this way can be just as effective as posting a picture of only your book. Think of it as subliminal messaging in a way; you want to remind readers about your books and expose them to new followers as well. You can also utilise days like 'Teaser Tuesday' or 'Work in Progress Wednesday' to talk about your books.

Do a Bookstagram Tour

Once you've built a relationship with other bookstagrammers, you can contact them with a request to participate in a promotional tour of your book. This can be casual, such as a request to post at any time during release week or even a cover reveal, or you can organise a tour with specific dates and requirements. There are also companies that host bookstagram tours if you don't have the time or know-how to go about hosting one yourself.

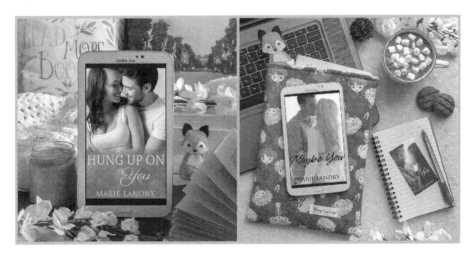

Other Perks of Being a Bookstagrammer

In the earlier 'Considering Your Audience' section, I talked about not expecting things in return. That being said, one of the perks of being a bookstagrammer is occasionally getting **free books** from other authors or even publishers. Sometimes this is a reciprocal agreement to promote each other's books and sometimes an author will simply send you a book because they think you'll enjoy it and hope you'll read it and leave an honest review.

With a bookstagram account, you also have the **potential to be a representative (rep) or influencer** for brands or companies. Many small bookish businesses depend on reps to help them spread the word about their products. In exchange for free merchandise, reps promote the company, share sales and promotions and get a discount code to share with their audience. For instance, in the last several years, I've been a rep for a candle company, two bookmark companies and a book sleeve company.

You also have the potential to do **sponsored posts and paid partnerships**. Some companies send free merchandise in exchange for promotion, while others pay you outright to promote their products.

Embracing the Wonder of Bookstagram

Bookstagram unites readers from across the world who share a genuine passion for books. It can be extremely valuable in connecting the literary community and helping to spread the word about indie books that may otherwise be overlooked.

For authors, it can be a fun and rewarding hobby. Many of us have trouble promoting ourselves and our books, even though it's necessary, and bookstagram is a way to do it in a way that feels more casual and natural.

About the Author
Marie Landry

Marie Landry's life revolves around books; when she's not writing them, she's reading them, taking pictures of them for bookstagram or blogging about them. An avid reader from a young age, she loves getting lost in characters' worlds, whether they're of her own making or someone else's. She particularly loves stories with as much of an emphasis on self-discovery and friendship as on romance...but don't leave out the romance!

She lives in a cosy apartment in Ontario, Canada with the best roommate ever, and can be found working in a room surrounded by Funko Pops and – you guessed it – books. When not doing bookish things, you can often find her cooking, exploring areas both familiar and new, watching TV or taking photos.

Marie writes heartfelt, hopeful romances that will make you laugh, feel and fall in love. To date she has released three books under the *Angel Island* series and six standalone novels: *Blue Sky Days*, *Hung Up on You*, *Maybe You*, *Mistletoe Kiss*, *Only You* and *The Most Wonderful Time of the Year*.

Connect Online
- **Websites**: www.marielandryauthor.com
- **Facebook**: www.facebook.com/MarieLandryAuthor
- **Instagram**: @sweetmarie_83
- **Twitter**: @SweetMarie83

Authorpreneurship
by Shauntay Dunbar

Going from Writer to Authorpreneur

A Little about Me

My name is Shauntay Dunbar, lovingly known as Shaunie to my family, friends and social media supporters. I am from the Bronx, New York and I am an author, podcaster, relationship expert, blogger, poet, speaker and event planner. Every time I get to talk about what I do for a living, I smile from ear to ear. If you had met me ten years ago and asked me where I saw myself in the future, my answer would have been completely different from the accomplishments listed above. I probably would have said something like, 'Married for twelve years, vacationing with our two children and...well, I don't really know what else.' Never in my wildest dreams would I think an annulment after almost three years of marriage, not having kids and getting back into the dating streets of New York City, would lead me to a path of happiness and authorpreneurship.

The Book That Started It All

My debut non-fiction book, *Diving in Stilettos First: Memoirs of Dating Mr. Right Now*, picks up where my marriage left off. Single again, in New York City in my 30s during the age of online dating and social media. It was my first time discussing my personal experiences 'out loud.' I'm a very private person and I initially worried that people might recognise themselves in the book and cause trouble. I quickly got over that fear when I made peace with the fact that this was my story to tell and I had healing to do through writing it. Plus, my lawyer said I would be fine!

In the book, I talk about rekindling old flames, online dating, being hooked up by friends and family, juggling multiple jobs and generally making time for everyone but myself. I was basically dating the same man in different forms. I had to take a step back and look at the common denominator in all the failed relationships: it was *me*. I needed to prioritise my life in order to attract what I really wanted – unconditional love. And I realised the best place to find that was to start with myself. Writing out my story was just the beginning of my self-awareness journey.

I've always loved writing, especially poems. Although, it wasn't until I finally quit working a second job and my co-worker asked me what I would do with my spare time that I decided picking up my writing would be a great space filler. So, I replied with my head held high, 'I'm going to write a book.' I had shared so many of my dating stories at work that people told me time and time again I should write one. So, I did, and after finishing the first chapter I felt so liberated I had to keep going. I had finally figured out what I wanted out of life. I wanted to do what made me happy and stop giving so much of my time working for someone else's dream. It was time for me to start working towards my own.

Naturally, I naively thought this book would instantly debut as a best seller, Oprah would call me for her book club and then I would take off to Hollywood for my movie premiere. Well, that didn't happen straight away, but my story isn't over yet. My success came in other ways and is still unfolding. I recently launched the audiobook and currently I am working on the screen play. Things may not happen the way you envisioned, but they happen in the way you need them to so you value victory when it comes your way.

Bringing the Book to Life

I finished writing my book in six months. Like many indie authors, I found innovative ways of fitting the time-consuming process of writing a book into my busy life, alongside a full-time job and hectic social life. I would write chapters in the notes section of my phone while on the train ride into work. Then I would email a draft to myself and continue writing on my lunch break, after work, at the gym and anywhere I felt inspired to write. It goes to show when you really want to do something, there is no perfect set up but you can make it work regardless.

Initially, I had a few trusted alpha readers who I shared early chapters with: my mum, a couple of cousins and a few friends who I knew would be honest with their feedback. Then my search for an editor began. It took me another six months to find an editor I trusted with my voice. That working relationship is crucial to a book's success, so it was incredibly important to me to find the right fit. In fact, this was one of many reasons I decided to self-publish. I wanted complete control regarding how my book was presented and when it would be released.

Many people think they have to network up the ladder in order to reach their goals, such as the mistaken notion that schmoozing with high-flyers will mean their success rubs off on you. In reality, I have found it much more effective to network across my peers. People who have specific talents will do things from the heart, take your work seriously and understand the experience grants them an opportunity to showcase their own creativity. I found my editor through a co-worker who happens to be a brilliant playwright. The illustrator of my book cover was a co-worker from my part-time job. I gave him some photos for an idea concept and he nailed it. Another co-worker helped with the fonts and cover layout of the book. Yet another co-worker helped me fine-tune my book blurb by offering constructive criticism. Needless to say, my book presentation was a community effort.

As first impressions are key for debut authors, I also invested money by printing 25 copies of my book and holding a focus group to see what people thought about it before I released it officially. The group gave amazing feedback and I was able to tweak the book accordingly to make sure my story didn't leave readers confused at any stage.

> **Top Tip**: It is helpful to make your book available in as many formats as possible, such as paperback, e-book and audiobook. This significantly expands your target audience of potential readers and means that you're not giving anyone a reason not to purchase your books because they only buy books in a certain format (such as audiobooks).

Building a Business around My Book

People who have read my book always tell me how relatable it is and how they went through similar situations or knew someone like me. In the three years following my book launch, I have attended numerous book fairs, got invited to speak at a wide range of events and have been interviewed on television, radio shows and podcasts.

Soon I found that people even started asking me for relationship advice and so I kept exploring ways to help people use self-love as one of many tools to find happiness again after a break up. Additionally, I began doing more collaborations, which took me out of my comfort zone and released some hidden talents I had no idea I possessed. I found that I really liked talking to people and helping them feel heard and inspired.

I enjoyed exploring these opportunities so much that I decided to create my own blog and began to incorporate funny skits, dating tips and relationship advice onto all my social media platforms. I also felt empowered to write poems and perform them during open mic nights, start a new podcast and so much more. Writing a book is not only therapeutic but it can also create multiple streams of income.

Top Tip: Always be yourself. When you speak your truth and are genuine, people can tell. They gravitate towards authenticity. This is important to bear in mind when thinking about how you present yourself on social media. There is a lot to be said for building your author brand around who you really are as a person, rather than attempting to portray yourself in a certain way.

Establishing My Author Brand

Getting Social with Marketing

One mistake many indie authors fall into is not thinking about how to promote their book until after it is available. Whereas to make maximum impact, it's best to start cultivating a loyal following long before your actual release date. Consequently, I started working on the marketing for my book months before I actually released it.

I built author social media profiles on Instagram, Facebook and Twitter centered predominantly on motivational quotes and relationship music. At the time, it was just as important to inspire me to keep going. Little did I know it was inspiring others to self-reflect and remove themselves from toxic situations and follow their dreams. This led to people asking me relationship questions, which in turn sparked a regular Instagram Live feature, 'Ask Shaunie', in which I encouraged my followers to interact and ask me questions directly. Clearly, I must have been doing something right because my Instagram profile alone reached over 10,000 followers in less than two years.

Book Signing in Style

Prior to releasing *Diving In Stilettos First*, I created an author website so people could get to know me better and I could provide the opportunity to purchase a signed copy. It also allowed me to set up my blog and create an email list to help keep in touch with my supporters, which has proved extremely valuable.

When it came down to my official book signing, I obviously imagined having it in a book store. One thing I have learned from my author journey is that God's plan is way better than my own. There is nothing traditional about me or my experiences. I was politely dismissed by numerous book stores because I was an indie author and didn't have a stronger social media backing or book store connection.

Remember when I said how important it is to network across your peers? Well, this is how I landed the iconic Lord & Taylor flagship department store in Manhattan for my book signing. I knew someone who worked for Estée Lauder and they thought it would be great to connect beauty with my book. I often spoke about 'date looks' in my book, so it actually made a lot of sense. They put me in touch with the department store and before I knew it, I had organised a book launch and signing at Lord & Taylor sponsored by Estée Lauder. We had swanky giveaways and the beautician team set up make-up stations to create 'date night looks' for my guests. It certainly provided an unforgettable experience and allowed me to make a great first impression as a debut author.

Always remember to be kind to people. As my experience has proved, you never know where friendships may lead. My favourite writer, Maya Angelou, famously said, 'I've learned that people will forget what you said, people will forget what you did, but people will never forget how you made them feel.'[40]

Seizing Every Opportunity

One incredible opportunity that came my way was my book being chosen for the book store at *Essence Fest 2018* in New Orleans. This three-day festival extravaganza routinely attracts over half a million visitors and celebrates black culture through music, film, art, food, fashion and empowerment.[41]

I was assigned an enviable spot right next to the main entrance. But I literally got the notice that my book was selected only two weeks before the show. I had to hustle. There was no way I was missing this opportunity. Happily, my mum's friend had recently moved to New Orleans and she was kind enough to let me stay with her while I did this three-day event. Direct flights were too expensive considering it was last-minute and it was over the Fourth of July weekend. So instead I flew into Houston where a friend picked me up from the airport and drove me to the bus station where I continued my long journey to New Orleans.

I was alone and nervous at the show, but I fought to get there so I gave it my all. I would spark conversation with attendees by doing what I do best: telling my story. As they entered the book store, I told people about my travels to get there and they purchased my book. It could be because they felt sorry for me, they were interested in the book, they enjoyed my personality, or perhaps all three. Either way, my book sold out on the first day.

---

[40] Carmine Gallo, 'The Maya Angelou Quote That Will Radically Improve Your Business,' *Forbes*, 31 May 2014, www.forbes.com/sites/carminegallo/2014/05/31/the-maya-angelou-quote-that-will-radically-improve-your-business

[41] '2018 Essence Fest Attracts over 500,000 Visitors to NOLA', *The New Orleans Tribune*, 11 July 2018, https://theneworleanstribune.com/2018/07/11/2018-essence-fest-attracts-over-500000-visitors-to-nola/

You Heard It Here First

Ever since I started considering different marketing methods, I knew I wanted to do an audiobook. One of my skills is doing funny voiceover skits that work well to engage people on social media and I thought it would be cool to hear my voice blaring from someone's car speaker.

As an indie author, you encounter two options when developing an audiobook. Hire a professional narrator, which can be very expensive, or go for the Do-It-Yourself option, which is considerably cheaper (or even free), albeit it takes significantly longer. However, because *Diving In Stilettos First* is a non-fiction book based on my own experience, I was the obvious narrator choice!

I worked with Contrackz Studio to painstakingly record every chapter until it was perfect and then, thirteen studio sessions later, the audiobook was complete. My studio engineer really did an amazing job. It was a steep learning curve for me and it was initially rejected twice by Audible because of technical formatting issues. Once I fixed those, my audiobook was officially released on 8 October 2019. The timing was actually perfect because my mum was diagnosed with a rare eye disease that is causing her to lose her vision. My book was the last book she could read and she loves it so much she was elated to hear it was on Audible and read in my own voice.

Stepping Outside of My Comfort Zone

Honestly, I struggled in the beginning when people would call me a relationship expert. I thought I had to have a therapist license and be certified in certain areas in order to be seen as a professional. But the reality is writing a book does make you an expert of sorts, you simply have to own it. My objective has always been not to tell people if they are right or wrong. Instead, I offer perspective on their situation so they can make the best decision for themselves. Every relationship is special, whether it is romantic or it is how you relate to friends, family or co-workers. What they all have in common is you. Your relationship with yourself is the most important factor because it affects everything else.

My book was not rated E for everyone. My target market was women aged 25 – 40 years old who have experienced heartache at some point in their dating life. I wanted to encourage them by showing you can find love again if you start by loving yourself. I created my blog, *Tales from the Single Relationship Expert*, to get people to laugh at themselves and embrace their single season. It's an ideal opportunity to learn and grow. The vicious cycle of dating toxic people has to stop and the only person you have control over is you, so why not start there. So, after a lot of soul searching, I embraced the relationship expert title that was given to me by my supporters and helped me launch my author brand.

Diversifying My Online Presence

After establishing my eponymous 'Ask Shaunie' social media feature, I went on to introduce 'Poetry Tuesday'. This embraced my love of poetry and provided another creative way to share what each chapter of *Diving In Stilettos First* was about. Over time, that led to 'Dating Tip Tuesday'. Ultimately, I want people to feel empowered to date while being the best version of themselves. So, I offer tips on how to achieve that every week, which has really resonated with my followers.

In my personal life, I have always had great discussions with my cousin about love and life, inevitably ending with a good laugh. She presented me with the idea of creating a podcast centered around debunking the myths surrounding dating and discussing various relationship topics, while ensuring the message of self-love, empowerment and positive mental health remained at the forefront. The pair of us took the plunge and started broadcasting on Instagram Live and now our *HerView* podcast has expanded to have four fabulous black women presenters and is streaming everywhere. Sharing content like this online has been really effective in sparking people's interest in my book and me as a person.

I have also been approached by numerous book clubs, which has led to lots of speaking engagements and live interviews with book club members. I've found this to be a really impactful way of connecting directly with my readers from all over the world and making myself more accessible as an author. Coincidentally, I met the leaders of the book clubs that I am part of myself by going to book fairs and book signings to show support for others, so this became a virtuous cycle that benefitted everybody.

Stepping into the Spotlight

Networking has been fundamental to my success as an indie author. Supporting other people and their ventures has given me the opportunity to connect and work with so many creative people. For example, a co-worker of mine started her own networking group and asked if I would do a speech. From there, I met more like-minded entrepreneurs who asked me to speak at their events and sell my books. I have even hosted a few events of my own in an eclectic mix of quirky venues, from gyms and salons to sneaker stores.

Remember how I spoke of kindness earlier? Well, a friend told me about an amazing woman, Danielle Jeter, who lived in Philadelphia and was making waves, huge tidal waves, in media. I reached out to her to share my story and send an Advanced Reader Copy (ARC) of my book prior to its official release. As a result, she invited me to be a feature author at her annual *Women in Media* global summit, which is a three-day conference that encourages women to own their voices and to utilise the power of their stories to advocate change.[42] The connections I made there are still solid to this day.

I have also been interviewed for numerous magazines, including *Essence Girls United, Da Culture, Epifiana, Align* and *Purposely Awakened,* as well as various podcasts and radio shows like *Hip Hop Point of View* and *Junk and Jam,* and even television networks. *Bronx Net TV* has invited me to be a guest on their show three times because who doesn't enjoy talking about relationships? Especially when the conversation is informative, engaging and fun. I have even been featured in the *Bronx Times* newspaper. I didn't see that coming.

---

[42] Visit www.womeninmediaglobal.org to learn more about this organisation.

It's All about Who You Know

Networking has also led to a plethora of collaborations. In *Diving In Stilettos First*, I mentioned how I would style my hair for certain outfits and, following a conversation with a friend of mine about this very topic, I applied to be a brand ambassador for Shea Moisture and have been successful every year since.

Through the *Women In Media* summit, I connected with a beautiful woman, Atiya Goldsmith, who was starting her own show called *Relationship Realness* and invited me to be her first guest. There I met the charismatic Chef Rashaun, owner of Infinite Catering, who was doing the cooking segment on her show. We had such a great time on set we all decided to stay in touch. Looking for a way to stay connected with our audience during the COVID-19 pandemic, we decided to collaborate together on a special virtual cooking show, *Ask Shaunie featuring Chef Rashaun*. He teaches everyone how to make delicious budget meals and I pose relationship questions to the viewers while they watch us cook. I have to say, my food presentation has gotten better with time.

People routinely reach out to me because they enjoy my social media content and my message of self-love. As a result, I now work with a few innovative apps: SuperShe, a she empowering network; Closurely, an app that helps people find closure after being ghosted and Green Light, a platform for creatives and influencers to connect with each other and form bigger networks.

Currently, I am also partnered with Fitline Health, Beauty and Fitness products. In my book I talked about how I got into running, and now I'm a cyclist too, so it is a mutually beneficial partnership. By sharing the importance of health, mind, body and spirit in parallel with relationship advice and promoting my book, I've been able to take my author brand to another level and uncover an exciting range of new opportunities. Focus on creating high quality social media content and people will seek you out and stick around. Just stay consistent and genuine.

> **Top Tip**: I cannot stress enough the importance of networking. If you want to get exposure for your book you have to go out and meet people. Apply to book events either as a vendor or as an attendee. Either way you have a chance to market your book, and you never know what new opportunities you might stumble across as a result.

Getting into My Stride

You never know where your next opportunity may arise from. After a chance conversation talking about my book and sharing dating stories with the owner of my gym, Fitness Sanctuary, she suggested that we host a joint event to promote healthy dating. I set it up and it was incredibly successful, bolstered by the fact it was located right in the heart of Time Square.

Another speaking engagement came from a friend who knew a professor in the liberal arts department at Mercy College. She purchased my book, loved it and invited me to speak about self-love and using your voice at the college in February 2020. Do you see how this works? Just be your authentic self and make meaningful connections. People will decide to do business with you because of who you are, not just what you do.

So, What Next?

I still have so many goals that I hope to achieve. I'm always striving to learn more and grow as a person. This helps me to continually expand my perspective and allows me to be more understanding. That movie premiere is coming, that Ted Talk is coming, another book is coming... But, most importantly, my ability to help more people learn to love themselves so they can love better is continually expanding as my author platforms grow. I believe in manifestation and so I am willing to do the work, stay consistent, help others along the way and let God lead it all.

Becoming an indie author has changed my life. I have tapped into buried talents, I have learned to operate extremely well outside of my comfort zone and I have met and been in rooms with people who I never thought I would rub shoulders with. Honestly, I feel free, possibly for the first time in my life.

A personal highlight for me is anytime I have been in front of a crowd and they were truly engaged in what I was saying. It makes me feel like my voice is finally being heard. I wish to help others feel the same. I have learned that living by faith is way more rewarding than living by fear could ever be.

To those who are new to writing or aspiring to be an author – stop aspiring and *go for it*. It will not be perfect; in fact, it will be downright messy at times. Inevitably, your book will not be liked by everyone and the beauty in that is it's not supposed to be. Celebrate what makes you different as an author and stop trying to get to the end result so quickly. One of the best things about being an indie author is that you are in charge of everything, so you can establish your own timeline and not have to rush things. Enjoy the lessons you learn along the way and the beauty of the writing journey. It will make for a pleasant, albeit crazy, ride. If you are anything like me, there will often be new challenges because you are always trying to better yourself. Embrace everything and keep moving forward. You can do this.

And who knows, writing your book might unlock opportunities that you haven't even dreamed of.

About the Author
Shauntay Dunbar

Shauntay Dunbar is an author, dating expert and entrepreneur from the Bronx, New York. She published her first book in 2017 titled *Diving in Stilettos First: Memoirs of Dating Mr. Right Now!* During the writing process she learned a lot about herself, calling it therapeutic. Readers connect with Shauntay and her journey because they either know a Shaunie or see themselves in her stilettos.

She continues to share her experiences while spreading her message of self-love via social media on her Instagram Live Show *Ask Shaunie with Chef Rashaun* and her 'Dating Tip Tuesday' feature will give insight and a good laugh. Her podcast *HerView* can be found on all streaming services and her blog, *Tales from the Single Relationship Expert*, is enlightening and informative. Shauntay has teamed up with brands like Estée Lauder, Lord & Taylor, Shea Moisture and *Essence Festival* to host event and speaking engagements across the country. Her first book was voted Favourite Read of 2018 by *Epifiana Magazine*, she was the feature author at the *Women In Media Philadelphia Conference 2017* and spoke at Mercy College in 2020.

Shauntay has done guest appearances on television and podcasts engaging in healthy conversations about love, life, dating, divorce and self-awareness. She is currently working on the screenplay and book number two, all while maintaining a day job as an event planner for a luxury publisher in New York City. Collaborating with other social media influencers and lifestyle experts to create online content and special events to empower women has become her passion.

Connect Online

- **Website**: www.divinginstilettosfirst.com
- **Facebook**:www.facebook.com/Diving-In-Stilettos-First-Memoirs-of-Dating-Mr-Right-Now-248760778956554
- **Instagram**: @diving_in_stilettos_first
- **Twitter**: @DiveNStilettos1

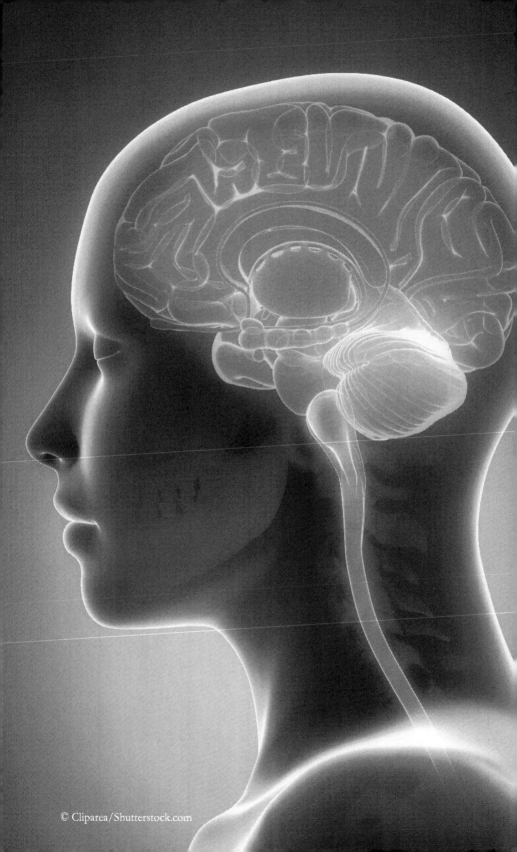

Encephalitis
by Samantha Goodwin

Why Are This Book's Profits Supporting Encephalitis?

Encephalitis was the devastating, little-known condition that claimed the life of my dad, Graham Finnerty, back in 2018. A great man, he had always dreamed of writing a book and sadly never got the opportunity to do so. In fact, he never even had the chance to read my own debut novel – but he did inspire me to write it in the first place.

As the creator who originated *Indie Writing Wisdom*, my hope is that his legacy will live on through all the writers who are inspired by this book and go on to release their own novels.

What Is Encephalitis?

If you have never heard about encephalitis, you are not alone. In fact, 78% of people worldwide do not know what encephalitis is.[43]

Encephalitis is an inflammation of the brain and it can affect anyone at any age. In the last decade, there have been approximately 250,000 patients affected by this condition in the USA alone, with potentially hundreds of thousands of cases worldwide every year. It is more common in many countries than motor neurone disease, multiple sclerosis, bacterial meningitis and cerebral palsy.[44]

---

[43] 'Encephalitis Facts & Figures,' *Encephalitis Society*, accessed 30 August 2020, www.encephalitis.info/facts

[44] 'What Is Encephalitis?' *Encephalitis Society*, accessed 30 August 2020, www.encephalitis.info/what-is-encephalitis

Encephalitis is caused either by an infection or through the immune system attacking the brain. It has a high death rate and survivors are often left with an acquired brain injury and life-changing consequences.

Possible symptoms to be aware of are:[45]

- Headaches
- Flu-like symptoms
- High temperature
- Seizures
- Confusion
- Uncharacteristic behaviour
- Memory loss
- Sensory changes
- Neck stiffness
- Sleep disturbances
- An altered level of consciousness

The Encephalitis Society

The Encephalitis Society, based in the UK, provides information and support to people affected by encephalitis and their families and friends. The charity also raises awareness of the condition, provides educational opportunities for health and social care professionals and conducts and promotes research.

All of the profits from e-book and paperback sales of this book will go directly to the Encephalitis Society to support their life-changing work. Thank you for helping us to support them.

Connect Online

- **Website**: www.encephalitis.info
- **Facebook**: www.facebook.com/EncephalitisSociety
- **Instagram**: @the_encephalitis_society_
- **Twitter**: @encephalitis

---

[45] 'What Is Encephalitis?' *Encephalitis Society*, accessed 30 August 2020, www.encephalitis.info/what-is-encephalitis

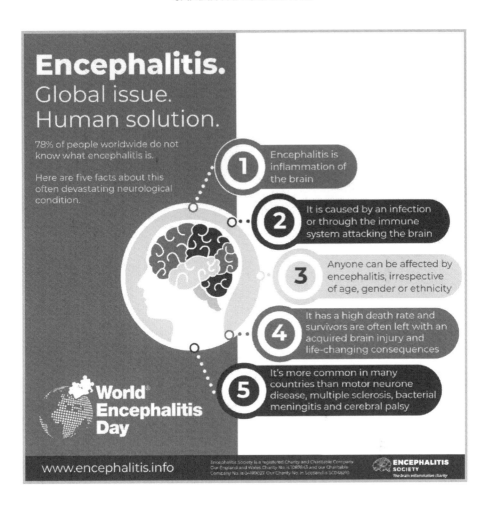

Acknowledgements
by Samantha Goodwin

Indie Writing Wisdom was a truly global collaborative project, and I am incredibly thankful for every single person who played a part in helping this book become a reality. There are a lot of people to thank, so here goes...

To every one of the contributing authors – you are all amazing and I feel so privileged that I had the opportunity to work with you on this. So, in 'order of appearance,' thank you to Stephen McClellan, Kara S. Weaver, Tempeste Blake, Angeline Trevena, Candice Bellows, Julia Scott, Michelle Raab, Holly Lyne, Marie Landry and Shauntay Dunbar.

Thank you to my husband, Chris Goodwin, for designing the beautiful book cover and supporting me throughout this whole crazy process.

Thank you to my incredible editor, Kelly Finnerty, for all the time you have invested to help refine this book and to my super-skilled proofreader, Claerie Kavanaugh (founder of Mirialis Editorial), for her expert eagle eye.

Thank you to Julia Scott (founder of Evenstar Books Design Services) for being my go-to consultant on the interior formatting of this book. Your expertise is so appreciated.

Huge thanks to all the fantastic beta readers, Felicia Blaedel, Donna H. Duhig, B.T. Keaton and Rebecka Yaeger (founder of Becka's Best Author Services), for your valuable feedback and providing your lovely review quotes.

A special thanks also to Tracie Daily for being an alpha reader of the 'Book Launch' chapter, and also Ricki Delaine, Cassidy Reyne and Kara S. Weaver for being alpha readers of the 'Book Marketing' chapter.

Thank you to the great ARC readers for sharing your thoughts after reading early copies of this book: J.D. Groom and S.M. Yair-Levy.

To all the bookstagrammers who contributed gorgeous original images for the different chapters – you have helped to make this book even more special and make it a true celebration of the indie book community. Thank you Katrina Botell (@rusticpages), Jenny DuRoss (@book-bookowl), Christina Dutting (@christina.marie.reads), Chloe Hodge

(@chloeschapters), Rebekah Hosford (@bekahsbookshelves), Marie Landry (@sweetmarie_83), S.M. Yair-Levy (@sm.yairlevyauthor) and Bridget (@darkfearietales_).

To my son, Jack Goodwin, thanks for just about keeping napping for long enough to allow me to pull everything together in those rare snatches of time! And thanks to Glynis Finnerty, Andrew Goodwin and Denise Goodwin for providing childcare so I could finish this project. Thanks also to my sister, Gillian Finnerty, for buying me the author notebook that instigated me to start writing this in the first place.

And to my dad, Graham Finnerty, thank you for inspiring this book.

Finally, thank you to all our readers for choosing to spend your time with this book. I hope you found it helpful. Always hold onto your dreams and never stop writing.

Enjoyed This? Leave a Review!

If you enjoyed reading *Indie Writing Wisdom*, please consider leaving a short book review online. It would be greatly appreciated and really does make a difference to indie authors:

- www.amazon.com
- www.amazon.co.uk
- www.goodreads.com

We all love connecting with our readers from across the world. Please feel free to share a photo on Instagram of you reading this book from wherever you travel or live.

Remember to use the hashtag *#IndieWritingWisdomWorldTour* and/or tag @samanthagoodwinauthor, and Samantha will happily repost (along with sharing some of your own work/photos if you wish).

Image Credits

Contents
- Main Chapter Image: © Janko Ferlic, @itfeelslikefilm/Unsplash.com
- Chapter-Header Circle Image: © Ana Tavares, @ana_tavares/Unsplash.com

Introduction
- Main Chapter Image: © Fotografierende, @fotografierende/Unsplash.com
- Chapter-Header Circle Image: © Milkovi, @milkovi/Unsplash.com

Motivation Matters
- Main Chapter Image: © Katrina Botell, @rusticpages
- Chapter-Header Circle Image, Author Photograph, Book Cover Images and To Dance Image: © Stephen McClellan, @stephenmcclellanbooks
- Girl Image: © Annie Spratt, @anniespratt/Unsplash.com
- Write Your Story Image: © July Milks/Shutterstock.com
- Create Something Today Image: © Paul Craft/Shutterstock.com

Plot Structure
- Main Chapter Image: © Rebekah Hosford, @bekahsbookshelves
- Chapter-Header Circle Image, Author Photograph and Book Cover Images: © Kara S. Weaver, @kara_s_weaver
- Lord of the Rings Image: © Rook76, rook76/Shutterstock.com
- Geisha Image: © John Cameron, @john_cameron/Unsplash.com
- Mountain Image: © Lucas Grey, lucasgrey/pixabay.com

Worldbuilding
- Main Chapter Image: © Savannah Yair-Levy, @sm.yairlevyauthor
- Chapter-Header Circle Image, Author Photograph, Book Cover Images and Maps Image: © Angeline Trevena, @angelineandtheworld
- World in a Book Image: © Mimma Key, HiddenCatch/Shutterstock.com

Characterisation

- Main Chapter Image: © Rebekah Hosford, @bekahsbookshelves
- Chapter-Header Circle Image: © Thought Catalog, @thoughtcatalog/ Unsplash.com
- Author Photograph and Book Cover Images: © Tempeste Blake, @tempesteblakeauthor
- Sherlock Holmes Image: © Ostill is Franck Camhi/Shutterstock.com
- Pride and Prejudice Image: © Elaine Howlin, @elaineh/Unsplash.com
- Earring Image: © Wonderlane, @wonderlane/Unsplash.com
- Scotch Image: © Johann Trasch, @cocktailbart/Unsplash.com

Editing

- Main Chapter Image: © Hannah Grace, @oddityandgrace/Unsplash.com
- Chapter-Header Circle Image: © Hannah Olinger, @hannaholinger/ Unsplash.com
- Author Photograph, Book Cover Image and Story Engineer Logo: © Candice Bellows, @storyengineer7
- Editor Definition Image: © Swellphotography/Shutterstock.com
- Editor Hand Image: © Andrey_Popov/Shutterstock.com
- Writing Image: © Kat Stokes, @katstokes_/Unsplash.com
- Crumbled Paper Image: © Steve Johnson, @steve_j/Unsplash.com

Cover Design

- Main Chapter Image, Chapter-Header Circle Image and all Book Cover Chapter Images: © Original Book Cover Designs, @originalbookcoverdesigns
- Final Full Page Image: © Susan Yin, @syinq/Unsplash.com

Formatting

- Main Chapter Image, Chapter-Header Circle Image and Bookstagram Images: © Chloe Hodge, @chloeschapters
- Author Photograph, Book Cover Image, Evenstar Logo and all other Chapter Images: © Julia Scott, @juliascottwrites

Book Launch Tips
- Main Chapter Image: © Christina Dutting, @christina.marie.reads
- Chapter-Header Circle Image, Author Photograph and Book Cover Image: © Samantha Goodwin, @samanthagoodwinauthor

Book Marketing
- Main Chapter Image: © Jenny DuRoss, @bookbookowl
- Chapter-Header Circle Image: © Campaign Creators, @campaign_ creators/Unsplash.com
- Author Photograph, Michelle Raab Marketing Logo, World Indie Warriors Logo, Marketing Formula Image and Sample Marketing Plan Image: © Michelle Raab, @michelleraabmarketing
- Marketing Image: © Rawpixel.com/Shutterstock.com
- Brand Image: © Constantin Stanciu/Shutterstock.com

Writing Community
- Main Chapter Image: © Bridget, @darkfaerietales_
- Chapter-Header Circle Image: © Green Chameleon, @craftedbygc/ Unsplash.com
- Author Photograph, Book Cover Images and all Chapter Images: © Holly Lyne, @hblyne

Bookstagram
- Main Chapter Image, Chapter-Header Circle Image, Author Photograph, Book Cover Images and all Bookstagram images: © Marie Landry, @sweetmarie_83

Authorpreneurship
- Main Chapter Image: © Katrina Botell, @rusticpages
- Chapter-Header Circle Image, Author Photograph, Book Cover Image and all Chapter Images: © Shauntay Dunbar, @diving_in_stilettos_first

Encephalitis
- Main Chapter Image: © Cliparea/Shutterstock.com
- Chapter-Header Circle Image and Encephalitis Image: © The Encephalitis Society/www.encephalitis.info

Acknowledgements

- Main Chapter Image: © Howie R, @howier/Unsplash.com
- Chapter-Header Circle Image: © Jaredd Craig, @jaredd_craig/ Unsplash.com

Image Credits

- Chapter-Header Circle Image: © Giannis Agathokleous, @giannis1992/ Unsplash.com

Printed in Great Britain
by Amazon